T0136407

Machine Learning and Optimization Models for Optimization in Cloud

Chapman & Hall/Distributed Computing and Intelligent Data Analytics Series

Series Editors: *Niranjanamurthy M and Sudeshna Chakraborty*

Machine Learning and Optimization Models for Optimization in Cloud

Punit Gupta, Mayank Kumar Goyal, Sudeshna Chakraborty, Ahmed A. Elngar

For more information about this series please visit:

https://www.routledge.com/Chapman--HallDistributed-Computing-and-Intelligent-Data-Analytics-Series/book-series/DCID

Machine Learning and Optimization Models for Optimization in Cloud

Edited by
Punit Gupta, Mayank Kumar Goyal, Sudeshna
Chakraborty and Ahmed A. Elngar

CRC Press
Taylor & Francis Group
Boca Raton London New York

CRC Press is an imprint of the
Taylor & Francis Group, an **informa** business
A CHAPMAN & HALL BOOK

First edition published 2022
by CRC Press
6000 Broken Sound Parkway NW, Suite 300, Boca Raton, FL 33487-2742

and by CRC Press
2 Park Square, Milton Park, Abingdon, Oxon, OX14 4RN

CRC Press is an imprint of Taylor & Francis Group, LLC

© 2022 selection and editorial matter, Punit Gupta, Mayank Kumar Goyal, Sudeshna Chakraborty, Ahmed A Elngar; individual chapters, the contributors

---

Library of Congress Cataloging-in-Publication Data

Names: Gupta, Punit, editor.
Title: Machine learning and optimization models for optimization in cloud /
edited by Punit Gupta, Mayank Kumar Goyal, Sudeshna Chakraborty, Ahmed A Elngar.
Description: First edition. | Boca Raton, FL : CRC Press, 2022. | Includes
bibliographical references and index. | Summary: "Cloud computing has
been a new trend in problem-solving and providing reliable computing
platform for big and high computational tasks. This technique is used
for business industries like banking, trading and many e-commerce
businesses to accommodate high request rate, high availability for all
time without stopping system and system failure"-- Provided by publisher.
Identifiers: LCCN 2021043504 (print) | LCCN 2021043505 (ebook) | ISBN
9781032028200 (hbk) | ISBN 9781032028248 (pbk) | ISBN 9781003185376 (ebk)
Subjects: LCSH: Cloud computing. | Machine learning.
Classification: LCC QA76.585 .M33 2022 (print) | LCC QA76.585 (ebook) |
DDC 004.67/82--dc23/eng/20211122
LC record available at https://lccn.loc.gov/2021043504
LC ebook record available at https://lccn.loc.gov/2021043505

ISBN: 9781032028200 (hbk)
ISBN: 9781032028248 (pbk)
ISBN: 9781003185376 (ebk)

DOI: 10.1201/9781003185376

Typeset in Minion
by Deanta Global Publishing Services, Chennai, India

Contents

Preface

CLOUD COMPUTING IS A new trend in problem-solving and providing reliable computing platforms for big and computationally intensive tasks. This technique is used for business industries like banking, trading and many e-commerce businesses to accommodate high request rates, high availability for all time without system failure. In case of failure, the requests are migrated to different reliable servers while letting the user know about it, providing the system with fault-tolerant behavior.

A new generation of computing optimization algorithms is also beginning with the introduction of machine learning and deep learning mechanism. The new generation of algorithms comes with new promises of improvement in existing models. Cloud and fog computing deals with many such optimization models which can be improved with increases in the performance of the system. The main aim of cloud computing is to meet the user requirement with high quality of service with the least computation time and high reliability. With the increase in services migrating over cloud providers, the load over the cloud increases, resulting in faults and various security failures in the system, resulting in decreasing reliability. The cloud system uses intelligent meta-heuristic and prediction algorithms to provide resources to the user in an efficient manner to manage the performance of the system and plan for upcoming requests. Intelligent algorithms help the system to predict and find a suitable resource for a cloud environment in real time with the least computational complexity taking into mind the system performance in underloaded and overloaded conditions.

Therefore, we have attempted to provide a significant effort in the form of the present book entitled *Machine Learning and Models for Optimization in Cloud*. The book contains 12 chapters.

Chapter 1 covers a general introduction to the multilayered architecture of cloud with its various service models. This chapter presents the cloud virtualization that is used to optimize the cloud services. It is the main sustaining technology in the cloud environment. Virtualization is accomplished with the help of virtualization software. This software separates a real calculating unit into several virtual ones; any device can be simply used and handled.

Chapter 2 discusses the responsibility of the cloud to manage the load over the existing infrastructure to maintain reliability and provide high-quality services to the user. Task allocation in the cloud is one of the key features to optimize the performance of cloud infrastructure. In this work, we have proposed a prediction-based technique using a pre-trained neural network to find a reliable resource for a task based on previous training and the history of cloud and its performance to optimize the performance in overloaded and underloaded situations. The main aim of this work is to reduce the faults and provide high performance by reducing scheduling time, execution time, average start time, average finish time and network load.

Chapter 3 focuses on task scheduling policy which aims to improve the performance in real-time with the least execution time, network cost and execution cost-effective at the same time. The proposed model is inspired by the Big Bang–Big Crunch algorithm in astronomy. The proposed algorithm aims to improve the performance by reducing the scheduling delay and network delay with the least resource cost to complete the task at least computational cost to the user with high quality of service.

Chapter 4 defines the role of service level agreements (SLA) in cloud. The SLA is a structured document specifying the needs of the consumer and the commitment of the provider for such services under conditions, and thus contains a collection of mandatory terms that must be met in order for the services to continue. Furthermore, the services offered by web services and those provided by the cloud are vastly different. The chapter discusses the role of SLA in cloud and its importance.

Chapter 5 discusses the role of deep learning and machine learning next-generation algorithms in cloud infrastructure for resource allocation. The chapter provides a review of existing models including nature-inspired algorithms, models using neural-inspired algorithms and meta-heuristic algorithms. A comparative study of existing work is showcased with issues in cloud. Finally, the chapter highlights this point and discusses various performance parameters regulating the performance of cloud.

Chapter 6 discusses versatility in cloud which is also known as scaling, which permits the provisioning and de-provisioning of processing resources of interest, through autoscaling. Auto-scaling strategies vary, and include different segments at the framework, stage and programming levels. Autoscaling likewise covers with other quality credits, in this way adding to support level arrangements, and frequently applies demonstrating and control methods to make the auto-scaling measure versatile.

Chapter 7 proposes a model that will focus on fault forecasting in tasks allocation. The projected model is based on a nature-inspired heuristic approach and intelligent artificial neural network. The fault-tolerant aware ANN-based proposed model focuses on performance improvement and reliability testing proactively. The proposed model surpasses the existing state-of-the-art methods for proactive and reactive fault-aware scheduling techniques in a large-scale data center. The results and discussions section supports the reliability assertion of the fault-tolerant aware human brain and nature-inspired model.

Chapter 8 has proposed an energy-efficient VM placement while improving several performance parameters using multi-objective optimization. Therefore, a backpropagation neural network–genetic algorithm (BPGA) model has been proposed that makes use of a non-dominated sorted genetic algorithm (NSGA) in the first pass and a backpropagation neural network in the second pass for the placement of virtual machines over physical machines. Compared with the traditional algorithms of VM placement, such as bin packing heuristics and other evolutionary algorithms, our proposed model shows better energy consumption with minimum SLA violation for the overall consolidation process. Furthermore, the proposed model also aims to minimize the overall cost of VM placement.

Chapter 9 focuses on energy efficiency in cloud data centers which is a very significant issue in the increasing use of cloud technology. A lot of work has been done to address the issue. Virtual machine (VM) consolidation is the key concept around which most of the research revolves. Meta-heuristic algorithms have a very important role in finding near optimal solutions for VM placement. This chapter presents a comprehensive classification of existing meta-heuristic algorithms. Finally a comparative analysis is performed for these algorithms to provide the researcher an insight into the area.

Chapter 10 details an energy-efficient hierarchical task scheduling algorithm for cloud to decrease the electricity consumption of the cellular nodes. The job is rescheduled when the node strikes past the transmission range. The overall performance is estimated primarily based on the common extend and packet shipping ratio based totally on nodes and flows. The overall performance metrics are analyzed with the use of an NS-2 simulator.

We hope that the works published in this book will be able to serve the concerned communities of optimization in cloud computing.

MATLAB® is a registered trademark of The MathWorks, Inc. For product information, please contact:

The MathWorks, Inc.
3 Apple Hill Drive
Natick, MA 01760-2098 USA
Tel: 508 647 7000
Fax: 508-647-7001
E-mail: info@mathworks.com
Web: www.mathworks.com

Editors

 **Punit Gupta** has been Associate Professor in the Department of Computer and Communication Engineering, Manipal University Jaipur, Jaipur, Rajasthan, India, from 2018. He received a BTech degree in Computer Science and Engineering from Rajiv Gandhi Proudyogiki Vishwavidyalaya, Madhya Pradesh, in 2010. He received an MTech degree in Computer Science and Engineering from Jaypee Institute of Information Technology (deemed university) in 2012 on 'Trust Management in Cloud Computing'. He is a Gold Medalist in MTech. He was awarded a doctoral degree in February 2017. He has research experience in the Internet of things, cloud computing and distributed algorithms and has authored more than 70 research papers in refereed reputed journals and international conferences. He is currently serving as a member of the Computer Society of India (CSI), a member of IEEE and a professional member of ACM. He has authored 15 books with Springer, IGI and many more.

 **Mayank Kumar Goyal** is an Assistant Professor at Sharda University, India. He received an MTech degree in Computer Science and Engineering from Jaypee Institute of Information Technology (deemed university) in 2012. He was awarded a doctoral degree in February 2019. He has research experience in the Internet of things, cloud computing and distributed algorithms and has authored more than 50 research papers in refereed reputed journals and international conferences. He is currently serving as a member of the Computer Society of India (CSI), a member of IEEE and a professional member of ACM.

Sudeshna Chakraborty has a consolidated 15 years of industry and academic experience. She is Research Group Head and Associate Professor of Computer Science in the Engineering Department at Sharda University, Greater Noida. She received a PhD in Computer Science and Engineering with Neural Network and Semantic Web Engineering.

She has acquired several awards for teaching, a research excellence award from the Institute of Scholars and an award for best paper presenter (IEI); she has been a keynote speaker, an organizing member of an international conference, a member of a reviewer committee, session chairs, Institute of Engineers, InSc and ATAL AICTE sponsored FDP and other FDP as a speaker. She has filed eight patents in the field of robotics, solar energy and sensors, chaired the IEEE conference in Paris ICACCE 2018 and was keynote speaker at the Springer conference in Tunisia ICS2A, Track Chair Smart Technologies and Artificial Intelligence Spain. She is an active member of professional societies like the IEEE (USA), IEI and IETA.

Ahmed A. Elngar is an Assistant Professor at the Faculty of Computers and Artificial Intelligence, Beni-Suef University, Egypt. He is Director of the Technological and Informatics Studies Center at Beni-Suef University. He is managing editor of the *Journal of Cyber Security and Information Management* (JCIM). The professor completed his Doctor of Philosophy (PhD) in Computer Science, Faculty of Science, from Al-Azhar University – Cairo, Egypt, in 2016. He has over 30 research contributions in reputed journals and conferences. He has also had 11 books published with reputed publishers.

Contributors

Deepika Agrawal
Department of Information
  Technology
National Institute of Technology
Raipur, India

Sneha Agrawal
Department of Information
  Technology
National Institute of Technology
Raipur, India

Amit Kumar Bairwa
School of Computing and
  Information Technology
Manipal University Jaipur
Jaipur, India

Sanjit Bhagat
Manipal University Jaipur
Jaipur, India

Surbhi Chauhan
Jaipur Institute of Engineering and
  Management
Jaipur, India

Vaishali Chourey
Department of Information
  Technology
Medi-Caps University
Indore, India

Mayank Kumar Goyal
Department of Computer Science
  and Engineering
Sharda University
Greater Noida, India

Punit Gupta
Department of Computer
  Communications and
  Engineering
Manipal University Jaipur
Jaipur, India

Sunil Kumar
Department of Computer
  Communications and
  Engineering
Manipal University Jaipur
Jaipur, India

Tarun Jain
Manipal University Jaipur
Jaipur, India

Jaya Krishna R.
School of Computing and
    Information Technology
Manipal University Jaipur
Jaipur, India

Dheeraj Rane
Department of Computer
    Science and Engineering
Medi-Caps University
Indore, India

Geetanjali Rathee
Department of CSE/IT
Jaypee University of Information
    and Technology
Waknaghat, India

Hemraj Saini
Department of CSE/IT
Jaypee University of Information
    and Technology
Waknaghat, India

Shally Vats
Department of Computer Science
Banasthali Vidyapith
Banasthali, India

Falguni Sharma
Manipal University Jaipur
Jaipur, India

Oshin Sharma
Department of CSE/IT
PES University
Bangalore, India

Sanjay Kumar Sharma
Department of Computer Science
Banasthali Vidyapith
Banasthali, India

Vijay Kumar Sharma
School of Computing and
    Information Technology
Manipal University Jaipur
Jaipur, India

Arjun Singh
School of Computing and
    Information Technology
Manipal University Jaipur
Jaipur, India

Devesh Kumar Srivastava
Department of Computer and
    Communication Engineering
Manipal University Jaipur
Jaipur, India

Rohit Verma
INSIGHT Research Lab SFI
Dublin City University
Dublin, Ireland

CHAPTER 1

Introduction to Virtualization in Cloud Computing

Vijay Kumar Sharma, Arjun Singh,
Jaya Krishna R, Amit Kumar Bairwa,
and Devesh Kumar Srivastava

CONTENTS

DOI: 10.1201/9781003185376-1

1.1 INTRODUCTION

Cloud computing involves centralized data storage policy. The client machine can access online cloud services or resources; hence, cloud computing can minimize user involvement. Figure 1.1 and Figure 1.2 depict the architecture and services of cloud computing. The cloud architecture includes hardware support like an advanced data center and cloud services [1]. Cloud service architecture has the following three layers:

a). Infrastructure-as-a-service (IaaS). This is located at the bottom layer, where physical (Emulab) and virtual (Google Apps, Amazon EC2) resources are handled as well as services in the form of network, storage and computing capability (Google's MapReduce). The grid computing is also referred to as IaaS, consisting of master and slave nodes. The master node distributes the workload, and the slave node runs the workload [1–3].

b). Platform-as-a-service (PaaS). This provides a development framework (Microsoft Azure) for programmers or helps developers to

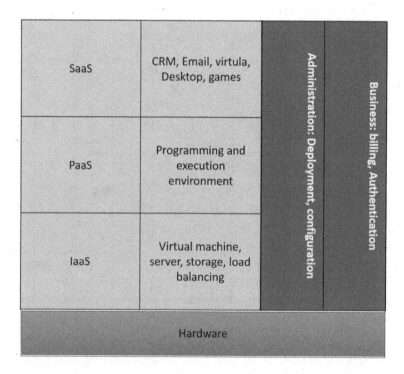

FIGURE 1.1   Architecture of cloud computing.

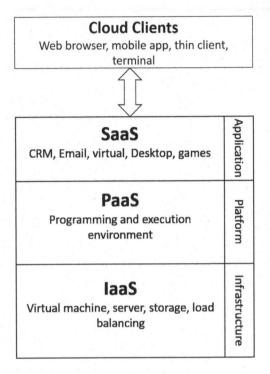

FIGURE 1.2   Services model for cloud to clients.

build software or functions on the platform of the provider. It's a fully virtualized network for one or several servers, particular applications and operating systems [1–4].

c). Software-as-a-service (SaaS). This is an application model (e.g., Google Apps model) in which software runs on the provider's infrastructure [1, 3, 4].

The following definitions expose the broader scope of cloud computing.

a. Cloud computing refers to a set of Internet-based applications that offer computational resources (service provider infrastructure, e.g., Google Apps, Salesforce.com) to end users. It may be hosted in a grid or utilities computing system, but it makes little difference to the service customer.

b. The cloud essentially refers to the transition from unstable local storage to stable scalable environments, from gigabytes of storage space (personal computer space) to an unlimited amount, and from

Microsoft Office to a web-based office. As opposed to storing locally on one's own server, the cloud makes online storage less costly and movement more stable.

c. The design of cloud computing can be typically broken into three sites:

- Providers. Cloud providers (Microsoft, Rackspace, Amazon EC2 Web Services) offer their infrastructure or platform for the users of the cloud environment.

- Enablers. These companies specialize in data center automation and server virtualization and provide the technology described above (VMware, Citrix, Redhat, Intel, Sun, IBM, etc.).

- Consumers. These are the businesses that make use of the resources and build or improve their web applications on top of the current cloud infrastructure.

1.2 CLOUD MODELS

Cloud services can be classified as public, private, community or hybrid [1, 2, 5, 6].

1.2.1 Public Cloud

When the services provided over a network are available to the public, the infrastructure is referred to as a 'public cloud'. Public cloud services can be available for free or on a pay-per-use basis [1, 3]. The services are dynamic, but they are accessible for self-service through the Internet. They are mostly handled by a large corporation (e.g., Amazon, Google App Engine).

1.2.2 Private Cloud

The cloud service in a private cloud is run solely by a single entity, whether it is handled internally or by another party [1, 4, 5, 7]. Private cloud ventures necessitate a substantial level and degree of meeting to virtualize the market climate, as well as a reassessment of current resource decisions.

1.2.3 Community Cloud

A community cloud is a form of cloud computing infrastructure that is shared by a group of organizations in a geographic region.

1.2.4 Hybrid Cloud

A hybrid cloud is a structure of two or more clouds that remain distinct entities but are linked together, allowing for multiple exploitation models to be used. The ability to seamlessly integrate and control applications using cloud infrastructure is a feature of hybrid clouds.

1.3 WHAT IS VIRTUALIZATION?

Today's exponential increase of data sharing across the network necessitates the use of programming models to execute programs through several distributed infrastructures. This increases the demand on the cloud resulting in heavy traffic load at the cloud network so we use virtualization to optimize the cloud services. Virtualization is defined in many ways; these are as follows:

According to Wikipedia 'Virtualization in cloud' is the construction of a virtual version (simulation of actual) of hardware or software resources (i.e., hardware platform, storage devices, operating system and so on). The concept of a virtual machine (VM) was introduced by IBM in 1960, to offer simultaneous, cooperating access of its mainframe computers. A virtual machine gives the illusion to the user that they can access the physical machine directly. While the virtualization principle improves the availability of CPU capacity everywhere in the world, the data that is executed on the client computer may be thousands of miles away, resulting in a delay in data fetch and execution. It maximizes resource usage while lowering costs.

Rune Johan Andresen defined virtualization as: Virtualization is a method of dividing computer power into different executable environments. More precisely, it is a software layer that gives several instances of VM the appearance of a real computer [8, 9].

Susanta and Tzi-cker describe it as: A technology that uses certain hardware and software partitioning methodologies to merge or separate resources to present one (e.g., desktop virtualization) or more operating systems [10].

IBM defined it as: It is the development of replacements for actual resources that execute the same functions and have the same external interfaces but differ in attributes (e.g., such as size, performance and cost) [11].

Andi Mann defined it as: Virtualization is a method of concealing the physical features of computer resources while allowing end users to communicate with them. Having a single physical resource function as several logical resources is an example of this [12].

William von H defined it as: Virtualization is the isolation of demand for real physical services on a continuous basis [13].

1.3.1 Benefits and Disadvantages of Virtualization

The following are the applications of virtualization, where the use of virtualization can be beneficial:

1. Multiple simultaneous operating systems (OS) [13, 14].

2. Testing [14, 15].

3. Server consolidation [12, 16, 17].

4. Virtual hardware [13].

5. Reduction in new hardware costs [13, 18].

6. Reduced downtime [15, 18].

7. Application consolidation [13–15, 19].

8. Better use of existing hardware [9].

9. Sand boxing [13].

10. Numerous execution environments [13].

11. Debugging [13].

12. Software migration [13].

13. Appliances [13].

14. Reduction in IT infrastructure costs [18].

The following are the disadvantages of virtualization:

- Information leakage issues [1, 13].

- The biggest disadvantage in virtualization is overhead, as it worsens performance [9, 13].

- The management of different platforms and networks is the biggest problem with virtualization as they in turn increase the time complexity of networking and debugging [9].

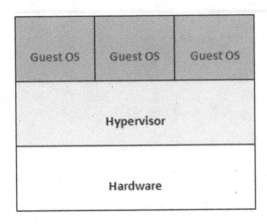

FIGURE 1.3   Virtualization architecture for cloud.

1.3.2 Virtualization Architecture for Cloud [3–6]

1. The OS takes full care of the underlying hardware.

2. A hypervisor/VMM in the virtualization architecture creates this illusion.

3. Virtualization is obtained with the help of virtualization software (i.e., hypervisor in Figure 1.3). Hypervisor is a software layer which:

a. Allows several guest OS (virtual machines) to run on a single physical host at the same time.

b. It can easily multiplex original hardware properties and offers hardware generalization to operating guest OSs.

1.3.3 Virtualization's Significance in Cloud Computing [7]

1. It is possible to have a cloud without virtualization, but it would be complex and expensive.

2. The cloud creates the ideas of 'pay for what you want' and 'infinite availability – use as much as you can'.

3. Only if there is a lot of versatility and reliability in the back-end are these ideas realistic. In virtualized environments, this efficiency is available.

4. Cloud computing is cost efficient when it uses virtualization.

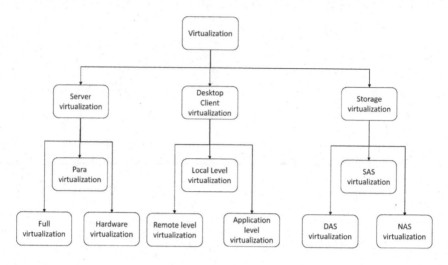

FIGURE 1.4   Virtualization types.

1.3.4 Classes of Virtualization and Its Effects

Server, desktop device and disk virtualization are the three forms of virtualization. The types of virtualization techniques are shown in Figure 1.4.

> **Class A: Server virtualization**: Through segmenting resources of individual servers through several networks, server virtualization enables a single server to handle the functions of several servers. The hypervisor layer provides this approach by using services in a cost-effective, highly accessible and efficient manner. Server virtualization can be categorized into three groups [20].
>
> a)   Full server virtualization.
>
> b)   Para server virtualization.
>
> c)   Hardware-assisted server virtualization.
>
> **Full server virtualization**: In full virtualization the VM gives the appearance of a virtual theater, on a physical machine within an isolated OS. For more secure and private computing the guest OS is separated from the hypervisor layer. Figure 1.5 depicts the full and para virtualization.
>
> **Para server virtualization**: In this virtualization, the guest operating system demands modification, to work with the hypervisor. This modified guest OS allows the hypervisor to more effectively

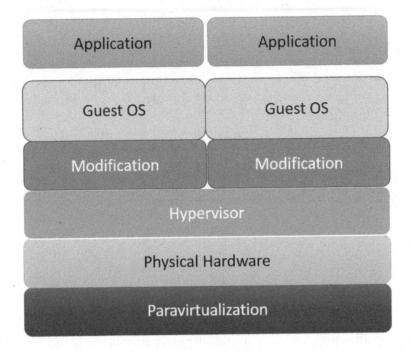

FIGURE 1.5   Full and para virtualization [20].

schedule computing resources to VM, to increase performance. Hardware and software requirements depend upon the hypervisor.

Advantages:

- It increases noteworthy performance over other virtualization techniques.

Disadvantages:

- Needs modification in VM OS.

Hardware-assisted server virtualization: Hardware manufacturers are rapidly introducing new features to make virtualization simpler. This form of virtualization was first used in IBM's VM/370 virtual machine, which was the first virtual machine. It accelerated the performance by reducing the maintenance overhead of the virtual machine, so this kind of virtualization is known as accelerated virtualization [21].

Advantages:

- Increase the performance.

- Products get distributed as a server OS or as a device.

Disadvantages:

- The vendor has to circulate a hardware compatibility list (HCL) in cloud that describes the hardware used with virtualization products [22].

Server virtualization has the following advantages [22]:

- Reduces the necessity for physical servers [23].
- Reduces server functioning maintenance [24].
- Reduces the operating expenditure [19].
- Reduces provisioning and the organizing of fresh services [24].
- Reduces disaster recovery times [19].
- Improves network and application security [25].
- Improves flexibility, availability and performance [25, 26].

Table 1.1 shows the comparative study of full virtualization, para virtualization and hardware-assisted virtualization, on different parameters.

TABLE 1.1   Comparison of Different Server Virtualization Techniques

Parameters	Full Virtualization	Hardware-Assisted Virtualization	Para Virtualization
Guest operating system modification	Unchanged guest operating system	Unchanged guest operating system	Changed guest operating system, so it cannot run on local hardware or another version of hardware
Performance	Good performance	Good and can also increase over time, depending upon hardware improvement	Better in certain cases
Used by	VMware, Microsoft	VMware, Microsoft, Xen	VMware, Xen, IBM
Dependency on guest OS hypervisor	No	No	Xen Linux runs only on Xen Hypervisor

TABLE 1.2   Comparison of Different Types of Hypervisors and Their Virtualization

| S. No. | Hypervisor Name | Types of Virtualization | | |
		Full	Para	Hardware-Assisted
1	KVM	Yes	No	No
2	Proxmox VE	Yes	No	No
3	Virtual Box	No	Yes	Yes
4	XEN	No	Yes	Yes
5	Open VZ	No	No	No

Table 1.2 shows different existing hypervisor names and their virtualization type.

Class B: Desktop or client virtualization [22]: This technology enables the system administrator to virtually update and monitor the desktop, mobile and laptop. There are many window manager programs based on X Window systems which are used to support multiple virtual desktop applications. These programs enable the user to switch between different desktops (e.g., mobile, laptop, computer desktop, etc.) and can display the output of specific applications [13]. Client virtualization is classified into the following three types:

1. Remote or server hosted virtualization: This is hosted on a server and managed by a network of clients.

2. Local client virtualization: The operating system is encrypted and virtualized, and it is run on a local desktop client. With the help of this kind of virtualization users are able to manage their desktop settings.

3. Application virtualization: This provides several ways to run applications on a single virtualized desktop machine.

The performance of desktop virtualization is affected in many ways as follows:

1. It depends on distance of line of business application given to a client from the head office.

2. Is it simplified management and reduced application lifecycle costs?

Desktop virtualization faces some problems which are classified as follows:

i. Application problems.

   – Slow performance of client/server applications in the network.

   – Remote access to applications.

   – Security of locally installed applications.

   – Incompatibility of co-resident applications.

   – Frequent application updates on hundreds or thousands of PCs.

   – Maintenance user data of the data center and not on the PC.

ii. Desktop problems.

   – Desktop lifecycle management cost.

   – Desktop management.

Class C: Storage virtualization: This is an emerging technology that simplifies storage administration and reduces the cost by producing a logical abstraction of existing physical storage, because the CPU generates the physical address of the storage unit, and then it is converted into a logical address. Storage virtualization provides abstraction of the logical address [9]. The following three varieties of data storage are used to provide storage virtualization.

a). **Direct attached storage (DAS)**: Storage drives are directly connected to the host computer in a DAS system.

b). **Network attached storage (NAS)**: This is a storage unit that connects the requesting machine to the server through the network.

c). **Storage area network (SAN)**: A storage unit is referred to as an SAN. It is used to exchange data between separate servers in order to speed up the network.

Storage virtualization is provided with the help of hypervisor software. Hypervisor can directly operate the hardware of the host computer.

1.4 CONCLUSIONS

Cloud computing is the demanding technology in today's digital world. The majority of users use cloud services because of their high performance and computation power. Many types of software are used to optimize the cloud; virtualization is one of them. Virtual machines are an essential and crucial part of cloud computing. By using several operating systems in isolated environments, these VMs minimize administration complexity. Without virtualization, the concept of cloud computing is feasible, but it would be inefficient and inflexible. Virtualization is an attempt to control the operating system.

REFERENCES

1. Y. Sharma, H. Gupta and S. K. Khatri, "A Security Model for the Enhancement of Data Privacy in Cloud Computing," 2019 Amity International Conference on Artificial Intelligence (AICAI), 2019, pp. 898–902.
2. J. Szefer and E. Keller, "Eliminating the Hypervisor Attack Surface for More Secure Cloud," 18th ACM Conference on Computer and Computer Security, New York, USA, 2011, pp. 401–412.
3. F. Wan, N. Chang and J. Zhou, "Design Ideas of Mobile Internet Desktop System Based on Virtualization Technology in Cloud Computing," 2020 International Conference on Advance in Ambient Computing and Intelligence (ICAACI), 2020, pp. 193–196.
4. Vijay Varadharajan and Udaya Tupkula, "Security as a Service Model for Cloud Environment," *IEE Transactions on Networking and Service Management*, Vol. 11, 2014.
5. Cong Wang and Sherman S.M. Chow, "Privacy-Preserving Public Auditing for Secure Cloud Storage," *IEEE Transaction on Computers*, vol. 62, 2013.
6. Claudia Canali and Riccardo Lancellotti, "Balancing Accuracy and Execution Time for Similar Virtual Machines Identification in IaaS Cloud," IEEE 23rd International WETICE Conference, 2014, pp. 137–146.
7. Durairaj M. and Kannan P., "A Study on Virtualization Techniques and Challenges in Cloud Computing", *International Journal of Scientific & Technology Research*, Vol. 3, 2014.
8. Rosenblum M. and Garfinkel T., "Virtual Machine Monitors: Current Technology and Future Trends," *Computer*, 2005, pp. 39–47.
9. Li Bignag, Shu Jiwu and Zheng Weimin, "Design and Implementation of a Storage Virtualization System Based on SCSI Target Simulator in SAN", *Tsinghua Science and Technology*, Vol. 10, 2005, pp. 122–127.
10. Susanta Nanda and Tzi-cker Chiueh, *A Survey on Virtualization Technologies*, Department of Computer Science SUNY at Stony Brook, 2012, pp.201–220.
11. IBM, *IBM Systems Virtualization Version 2 Release1*, International Business Machines Corporation, 2005.

12. Andi Mann, *Virtualization 101: Technologies, Benefits, and Challenges*, Enterprise Management Associates, Inc. 2006.
13. William von H., *Professional Xen Virtualization*, Wiley Publishing, Inc., 2008.
14. Qian Lin, Zhengwei Qi, Jiewei Wu, Yaozu Dong and Haibing Guan, *Optimizing Virtual Machines Using Hybrid Virtualization*, Elsevier Inc., 2012.
15. Jeanna N., Eli M., Todd D., Wenjin H., Jeremy B., Patrick F. and Brendan J., *Running Xen: A Hands-On Guide to the Art of Virtualization*, Prentice Hall, 2008.
16. B. Harris and N. Altiparmak, "Monte Carlo Based Server Consolidation for Energy Efficient Cloud Data Centers," 2019 IEEE International Conference on Cloud Computing Technology and Science (CloudCom), 2019, pp. 263–270.
17. Jeanna N., Eli M., Todd D., Wenjin H., Jeremy B., Patrick F. and Brendan J., *Running Xen: A Hands-On Guide to the Art of Virtualization*, Prentice Hall., 2008.
18. Serjeant A., "Building a Case for Server Consolidation," *VM World.* Presentation, Oct. 2005.
19. HP, *Server Virtualization Technologies for x86-based HP Blade System and HP Pro Liant Servers Technology Brief*, 3rd edition, Hewlett-Packard Development Company, L.P., 2009.
20. Matthew Overby, *A Survey of Virtualization Performance in Cloud Computing*, University of Minnesota Duluth, 2014.
21. Keith Adams and Ole Agesen, "A Comparison of Software and Hardware Techniques or x86Virtualization", ACM, San Jose, CA, October 21–25, 2006.
22. Radhwan Y Ameen and Asmaa Y. Hamo, "Survey of Server Virtualization", *International Journal of Computer Science and Information Security*, Vol.11, No. 3, 1–10, 2013.
23. Wolf C. and Halter E., *Virtualization from the Desktop to the Enterprise*, Apress, 2005.
24. VMware, *Reducing Server Total Cost of Ownership with VMware Virtualization Software*, VMware, Inc., 2006.
25. Ravi G Singh, *Server Virtualization and Consolidation: A Case Study*, IBM Corp., 2007.
26. IBM, *IBM Systems Virtualization Version 2 Release 1*, International Business Machines Corporation, 2005.

CHAPTER 2

Machine Learning, Deep Learning-Based Optimization in Multilayered Cloud

Punit Gupta and Mayank Kumar Goyal

CONTENTS

DOI: 10.1201/9781003185376-2

2.1 INTRODUCTION

In this generation of growing need for fast computing power, cloud computing is the best solution to fulfill the upcoming needs and manage the performance of the data centers at the same time. The resource allocation in a cloud computing environment depends on resources used, cost of resources and scheduler policy to improve the performance of the system. The local or global optimal point provides the solution [1, 2]. User requirements may test directly on a real cloud computing environment, but this increases the overhead costs; for example, Microsoft Azure and Amazon EC2 provide real test environments. The scalable simulation reduces the cost. Cloud computing provides dynamic services using virtual resources over the Internet [2]. Several reactive techniques are presented in the literature review for handling the failure rate of cloudlet execution on reliable and unreliable virtual machines. Hence in our research work, we are focusing on a cost-efficient proactive fault-tolerant strategy. It includes predictive, criteria-based policy respectively. These approaches focus on historic logs, heuristic, meta-heuristic and single-objective and multi-objective allocation with high reliability. Our focus area includes predictive-based proactive fault-tolerant aware scheduling in a cloud [2]. Charity et al. focused on proactive approaches for resource reliability including the configuration parameters of computing, storage and network resources [3–6].

C. Zhao et al. demonstrated bio-inspired strategies, which reduce the over resource provisioning overhead. The authors focused on independent task mapping using a bio-inspired genetic approach [4].

In this article, we introduce a proactive, predictive power-aware fault-tolerant efficient scheduling technique which is based on a hybrid approach using the BB–BC algorithm and feedforward neural network. This is also known as fault-tolerant ANN (Artificial Neural Network) based scheduling. Results demonstrate that the proposed technique improves the reliability of the virtual machines.

2.2 RELATED WORK

Cloud computing is a promising option for modern industries to achieve high performance at affordable cost with a scalable and flexible environment. In the real world cloud is a heterogeneous combination of various services providing various storage, networking and processing services to the user on a pay-per-use model. Cloud computing is responsible for executing the user task with high computation and the least cost as promised to the user without compromising on either quality matrix [7–10]. To manage these tasks scheduling plays an important role in improving the performance of the cloud and quality of service to users.

S. G. Damanal et al. [11] revealed the status of the virtual machines in a cloud computing environment. The authors have also considered the active load balancer as the key focus area of the work. There is scope to implement the policy which supports the dynamic environment and scalable simulation. Researchers described the load balancing scheme for the private cloud. The performance measurement criteria include utilization standards. The authors primarily focused on bio-inspired meta-heuristic techniques for the performance measurement of the scalable cloud [12]. The authors have considered nature-inspired ant colony optimization and particle swarm optimization techniques for the quality of service improvement [13, 14]. Kalra et al. proclaimed a survey on meta-heuristic algorithms [15]. Beheshti Z. et al. explained the population-based meta-heuristics algorithms for cloud scheduling which include genetic algorithms, PSO, ACO and many more [16–19]. The author also presented the various optimization criteria for the optimal global solution.

Genez et al. [20] presented a workflow scheduler in a hybrid cloud using performance metrics makespan, cost and bandwidth. H. R. Faragardi et al. [21] presented a novel resource provisioning mechanism for workflow scheduling. The performance is measured using performance metrics makespan on the IaaS cloud. Q. Wu et al. [22] modeled the multi-objective evolution-based scheduling technique and focused on the simultaneous optimization of makespan and economical cost. V. Arabnejad et al. [23] introduced a budget deadline-aware scheduling technique. The authors also studied the novelty of the proposed technique using sensitivity analysis. S.K. Mishra et al. [24] focused on two levels of provisioning in the scalable cloud scenario. The provisioning covered task to virtual machine mapping and virtual machine to host mapping. The performance is measured using power consumption. N. Mansouri and M. M. Javidi [25] proposed a job type- and cost-based job scheduling technique. The performance is measured using the response time of the data-intensive and computing-intensive jobs. Y. Lu and N. Sun [26] proposed a resource-aware load balancing based task scheduling technique. The optimization metrics included, e.g., power saving and resource utilization. The proposed technique supports the green computing environment. Our primary objective focuses on power saving, time and costs trade-off in a cloud computing environment using a constant IaaS cloud. In this section, a detailed review has been given [27–31]. It discusses the existing techniques for task mapping on virtual machines and various parameters are used for quality of service measurement. The nature-inspired meta-heuristic techniques are reviewed which focus on performance metrics, power saving, response time and temperature awareness using datasets. This section also reveals the disadvantages of existing methods of finding a global solution from algorithms like the genetic and Big Bang–Big Crunch algorithms, which are costly in terms of scheduling time, which increases with the increase in problem size.

2.3 PROPOSED METHODOLOGY

The algorithm works on the fundamentals of Big Bang–Big Crunch-based optimization and artificial neural networks.

The proposed model uses the tasks list and virtual machine list as an input to the model. The proposed model is divided into the following phases:

1. Initialization.

2. Dataset preparation.

3. Model preparation.

4. Training.

5. Backpropagation.

6. Task scheduling.

2.3.1 Initialization

In this module, all the parameters like the number of input layers, hidden layer and output layer are defined with several neurons in each layer: Learning Rate, Mutation Rate, Population Size, Evolution, Neurons Input Layer, Neurons Output Layer, Neurons Hidden Layer, Activation Function. This phase defines the efficiency and accuracy of the proposed model using these parameters.

2.3.2 Dataset Preparation

In this phase, the dataset for the training phase is prepared using a Big Bang–Big Crunch algorithm with average VM utilization, network delay and execution time as a fitness function to improve the network, power efficiency and makespan at the same time. The complete algorithm is discussed in Section 2.3.1. This phase takes a list of tasks, which is a heterogeneous combination of a variety of tasks along with a list of virtual machines available as resources. The input is given to the proposed modified BB–BC algorithm. The algorithm is designed to find a global optimum solution in the least number of evolutions and mutations. The proposed power- and network-aware model takes care of both network delay and utilization of the resources to improve the power consumption of the system.

$$\text{fitness\_value}_i = \sum_{j=1}^{j=n} (\alpha * \text{Network\_cos}t_j + \beta * \text{Completion\_time}_j \qquad (2.1)$$
$$+ \gamma * \frac{1}{\text{Failure\_rate}_i})$$

Where $\alpha + \beta + \gamma = 1$.

$$\text{Total\_Execution\_time} = \sum_{i=1}^{n} \text{Task\_Length}_i / \text{MIPS}_j \qquad (2.2)$$

Equation 2.1 denotes the linear weight function with weight factor α for network cost and weight factor β for total execution time respectively. The execution time is measured using Equation 2.2.

2.3.3 Model Preparation

In this module, a neural network is designed using parameters for the initialization phase. The model consists of the input layer, hidden layer and output layer with activation function; the input later and hidden layer adjust the weight in such a way that the output of the network is similar to the expected output of the training dataset.

The output of an adaptive two-layer perceptron model presents the virtual machine identity which handles the user requests. It uses a feedforward and backpropagation method for achieving the target values. The three-layer artificial neural network-based model improves the performance of the astronomy-inspired genetic algorithm. The artificial neural network trains using different learning rates. The accuracy of the output depends on training parameters. The network has several layers and several nodes in each layer. The performance is affected by the training mechanism.

2.3.4 Training

In this phase, the designed neural model is trained with 80% of the training data prepared in the training dataset preparation phase. The phase is important because it is responsible for setting the weights of the neural network which defines the accuracy of the neural network.

The training process initializes the weight and bias parameters. The process recurs until the target values are attained. The target values of the proposed model include the instance identity, which takes minimum makespan for the completion of the tasks. The training process predicts an appropriate value of the unknown variables. The training mechanism includes the error correction-based mechanism and memory-based mechanism. The optimal trained neural network provides the optimal global solution with accuracy, stability and correctness. The available data should be categorized by applying a rule of thumb, i.e., 80% of available data is used for training, and the rest of the data is used for validation of output. The activation function Leaky ReLU is used at hidden layers and the sigmoidal function is used at the output layer.

2.3.5 Backpropagation and Error Correction

Here the objective of this phase is to improve the accuracy of the neural network by adjusting the weights of the neurons at the input layer and hidden layer to achieve the desired output.

The proposed model follows the error correction learning mechanism. The error correction learning mechanism improves the quality of service using the cost function (δ_k). The goal is to minimize the cost function using the signal flow graph of the ANN model as shown in Figure 2.1. The error correction learning mechanism measures the error using Equation 2.3.

$$e_k(n) = d_k(n) - y_k(n) \tag{2.3}$$

$$\delta_k = \frac{1}{2} * e_k^2(n) \tag{2.4}$$

In Equation 2.3, and Equation 2.4, the parameter $d_k(n)$ denotes the expected output, $y_k(n)$ denotes the exact output and $e_k(n)$ is the error, and δ_k is the cost function used in the learning process of the ANN model respectively.

2.3.6 Task Scheduling

In this phase, the perceptron model with appropriate training is used for task scheduling to improve the scheduling time, power efficiency and total execution time of the tasks.

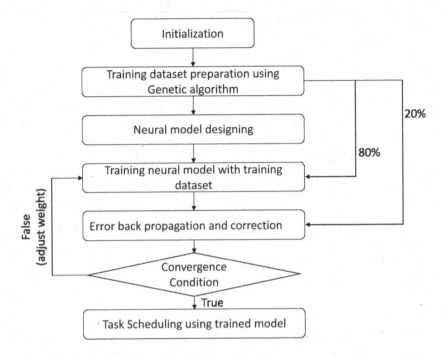

FIGURE 2.1   Flow diagram of the proposed BB–BC ANN scheduling technique in cloud.

2.3.7 Steps of Big Bang–Big Crunch

The proposed algorithm considers that a cloud is a heterogeneous combination of various services providers which provide services with varying cost, resources and performance. Cloud controller and task scheduling policy is responsible for finding a suitable resource on a service provider to complete the task in the least time and execution cost and with a defined quality of service. The proposed algorithm is meant to cover all the performance parameters discussed above.

The proposed algorithm is divided into four modules:

Module 1: Initialization/population generation.

Module 2: Fitness evaluation.

Module 3: Crossover/center of mass + mutation.

Module 4: Big Crunch.

2.3.7.1 Phase 1: Initialization/Population Generation

In this phase, initialization of population and other basic parameters is done, where the population is considered as a completed schedule consisting of tasks which are generated using Poisson distribution because the task occurrence is completely random in the real world. The function of probabilistic distribution is given below in Equation 2.8.

$$p(X = x) = \frac{\lambda^x e^{-\lambda}}{\lfloor x} \quad \text{where } x = 0, 1, 2, 3 \ldots\ldots \quad (2.5)$$

Where x is a natural number showcasing the population size, i.e., the number of tasks. λ is the rate of requests arriving which is usually greater than zero. In this phase, 'p' populations are initialized with random VMs being allocated to the task. The populations finally constitute a predefined set of randomly generated tasks and each in a population is initialized with random VM IDs. After this phase, the fitness value for each population is initialized which defines the performance and quality of service of each schedule.

2.3.7.2 Phase 2: Fitness Evaluation

This phase starts with the evaluation of the fitness value of each population as given below. Fitness plays an important role in identifying whether the schedule will take part in the next generation of evolution or not. Fitness in BB–BC is also referred to as the mass of the schedule. In the proposed algorithm the fitness function is defined as follows:

fitness value$_i$ is defined as the fitness of the ith population, where the fitness function is the sum of cost and execution of each task over a VM where j states the number of tasks.

Where $\alpha + \beta = 1$.

$$fitness\_value_i = \sum_{j=1}^{j=n} (\alpha * Network\_cost_j + \beta * Completion\_time_j \quad (2.6)$$
$$+ \gamma * \frac{1}{Failure\_rate_i})$$

The task completion time variable is measured using Equation 2.6 in which Task_Length is the number of instructions of a task, VM_MIPS is the millions of instructions per second (MIPS) of VM and PE is the processor count.

$$Network\_cost_i = Network\_delay_i \quad (2.7)$$

$$Failure\_rate_i = \frac{task\_failed\_count_i}{\Delta T} \tag{2.8}$$

The simulation of failure depends on the probabilistic distribution function. Task_failed_count concerns measures over a period of time ΔT.

Equation 2.7 defines the cost of resources used during the execution of a task at a specific VM. In this phase, the mass of all the schedules is evaluated and then evolution takes place. Evolution is a set of steps repeated in every evolution which include selection, crossover, mutation and the big crunch phase.

2.3.7.3 Phase 3: Crossover/Center of Mass and Mutation

In this phase two best solutions are selected. The first solution is the one with the least cost, and the second solution is the one with the fitness value near to the center of mass of all the solutions, where the center of mass is evaluated using Equation 2.9. The center of mass refers to the average solution or the mean position in the solution which is considered to be the most stable as compared to the best and worst solutions. The center of mass is referred to as x^c.

$$x^c = \frac{\sum_{i=1}^{i=N} \frac{1}{f_i} x_i}{\sum_{i=1}^{i=N} \frac{1}{f_i}} \tag{2.9}$$

x^c is a point in n-dimensional space where N is the number of populations. f_i is the ith solution in N-dimensional space. The second fittest solution is the solution nearest to the center of mass, i.e., the solution having a fitness value near to the center of mass.

2.3.7.3.1 Crossover This phase takes two best solutions from the selection phase and a multi-point crossover is performed in which the swapping of a random point between two solutions selected is done. This phase aims to design a better solution from the two best solutions.

2.3.7.3.2 Mutation In this phase, the third-best solution discovered spreads its diversity in other populations using swapping-based mutation of the candidate solution in a search space with other solutions.

2.3.7.4 Phase 4: Big Crunch

This phase plays an important role by removing the population with the worst fitness value, i.e., the highest fitness value. Repeat phases 2, 3 and 4 until one best solution is left.

Figure 2.3 presents the flow diagram of the proposed model.

2.4 EXPERIMENTAL RESULT

In this work, we focus on performance enhancement using an astronomy-aware and human brain-inspired approach. In this section, the performance evaluation of the proposed model is performed. Many criteria are used for task scheduling evaluation. Many of the Metrics are given below:

- Average start Time (millisecond).

- Total execution time/makespan (millisecond).

- Average finish time (millisecond).

- Network delay (millisecond).

2.4.1 Results Using Fabricated Data

This subsection illustrates the results with scaling load to study the performance in underloaded and overloaded conditions. Figures 2.2(a) and (b) show the comparisons of the variations of the execution time with scaling tasks and resources. The astronomy-aware and human brain-inspired BB–BC ANN performs better than state-of-the-art approaches. Figures 2.3(a)

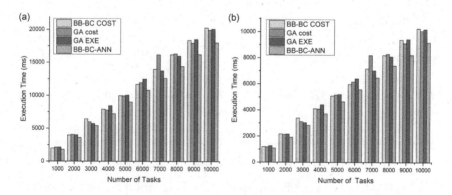

FIGURE 2.2   (a) Comparison of execution time with five virtual machines. (b) Comparison of execution time with ten virtual machines.

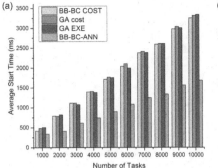
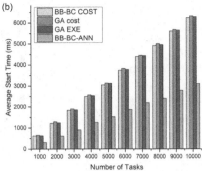

FIGURE 2.3   (a) Comparison of average start time vs scaling tasks with five virtual machines. (b) Comparison of average start time vs scaling tasks with ten virtual machine.

and (b) show the BB–BC ANN with variations of the average start time with scaling tasks and resources.

Figures 2.4(a) and (b) show the study of the task failure count on increasing the user tasks with five and ten virtual machines. Figures 2.5(a) and (b) show the study of the task completed count on increasing the user tasks with five and ten virtual machines. Figures 2.4 and 2.5 show that the proposed algorithm performs better in a fault environment with more tasks completed as compared to existing algorithms.

Figures 2.6(a) and (b) exhibit the results which are computed with increasing task load and scaling the resources in terms of a virtual machine. The proposed algorithm performs better as compared to existing approaches to in-network and fault-aware environments.

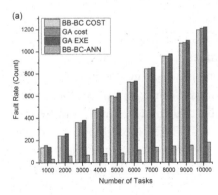
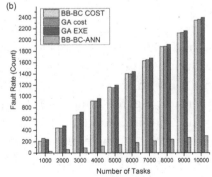

FIGURE 2.4   (a) Task failure count with five virtual machines. (b) Task failure count with ten virtual machines.

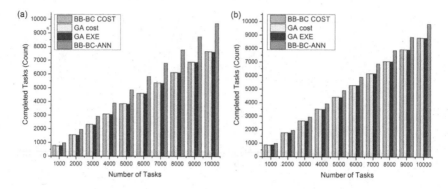

FIGURE 2.5 (a) Task completed count with five virtual machines. (b) Task completed count with ten virtual machines.

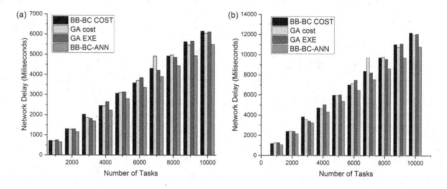

FIGURE 2.6 (a) Comparison of network delay with five virtual machines. (b) Comparison of network delay with ten virtual machines.

2.4.2 Experimental Results Using Real Datasets

In this section, the simulation is performed using a real dataset from a parallel workload using datasets. All the simulations listed below are performed with scaling five and ten machines. The performance is evaluated with increasing load, i.e., the number of tasks. The comparison is carried out with existing BB–BC cost, and two other variants of the genetic approach. Figures 2.7(a) and (b) exhibit that the tasks are submitted on virtual machines using the proposed BB–BC ANN, BB–BC cost and two other variants of the genetic approach. The performance is measured using the average start time. Figures 2.8(a) and (b) exhibit the variations of the average finish time using the proposed BB—BC ANN and state-of-the-art existing approaches. The average finish time acts as a performance metric. Figures 2.9(a) and (b) show the comparative results over execution time

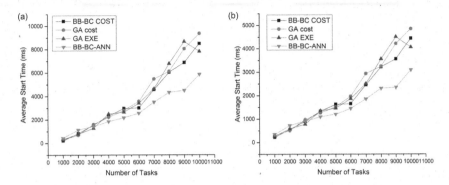

FIGURE 2.7 (a) Comparison of average start time vs five virtual machines. (b) Comparison of average start time vs ten virtual machines.

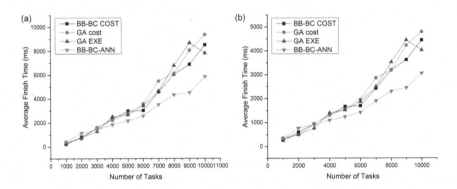

FIGURE 2.8 (a) Comparison of average finish time vs five virtual machines. (b) Comparison of average finish time vs ten virtual machine.

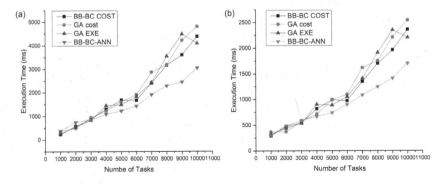

FIGURE 2.9 (a) Comparison of execution time vs five virtual machines. (b). Comparison of execution time vs ten virtual machines.

TABLE 2.1   Simulation Parameters

Hyper parameters	Hidden layer:1, hidden units = 3, Learning rate = 0.2
Mutation rate	0.15
Evolution	100
Population size	100
Number of hidden layers	3
Neurons in output layer	50/100
Neurons in each hidden layer	50
Activation function	Leaky Relue Activation function =
	$f(x) =$
	$\{\alpha * x \text{ if } x \leq 0, x \text{ if } x > 0\}$
	$\forall\ \alpha = 0.01$

as a performance matrix. The results are computed with increasing task load and scaling the resources in terms of the virtual machine (Table 2.1).

The prosed algorithm performs better as compared to existing approaches to in-network and fault-aware environments.

Figures 2.10 (a) and (b) show the comparative results over the number of tasks completed as a performance matrix. The results are computed with increasing task load and scaling the resources in terms of the virtual machine. Figures 2.11 (a) and (b) show the comparative results over the number of tasks failed as a performance matrix, where the fault in the system occurs randomly using Poisson distribution. This performance matrix shows that the proposed algorithm reduces the network load and execution time as shown in Figure 2.12 which improves the system performance and quality of service as compared to existing algorithms. Figure 2.12

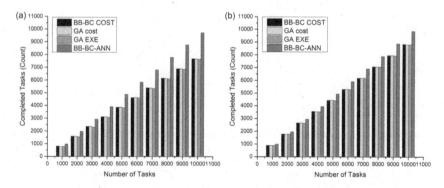

FIGURE 2.10   (a) Comparison of task completed count vs five virtual machines. (b) Comparison of task completed count vs ten virtual machines.

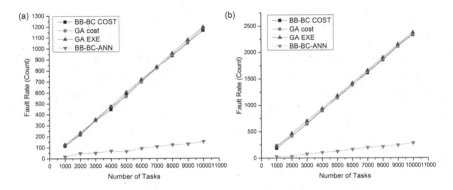

FIGURE 2.11 (a) Comparison of task failure count vs five virtual machines. (b) Comparison of task failure count vs ten virtual machines.

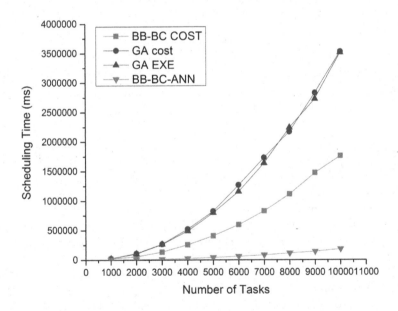

FIGURE 2.12 Comparison of simulation time vs five virtual machines.

shows the comparative results over simulation time in milliseconds as a performance matrix. The results are computed with increasing task load the performance of the proposed BB–BC ANN improves as compared to the traditional algorithm because the traditional algorithm needs a large number of iterations to find the best solution whereas the proposed algorithm is a trained neural network which needs to be trained once for a scenario.

2.5 CONCLUSION

This work presented an astronomy- and neural-inspired virtual machine assignment to the user requests approach based on the features of the human brain and optimization method. The proposed algorithm tries to improve the fault tolerance of the cloud environment and to improve the performance of the system at the same time using machine learning techniques. The results and discussions section illustrates that BB–BC ANN performs better than existing meta-heuristic techniques. The study of the proposed algorithm is performed with scaling task load and resources. Future work may focus on virtual machine allocation in a data center network. The drawback of the proposed algorithm is that the neural network needs to be trained after some time with updated upcoming tasks to overcome the decay of the trained model. This training time will, however, be much shorter than the total sum of the simulation time of the existing algorithm. In the future, the algorithm may improve the power consumption and scalability in the cloud environment. The proposed algorithm proved to perform better in the COVID-19 situation with overloaded and underloaded conditions in the cloud and performs better than any existing algorithm in both underloaded and loaded conditions.

REFERENCES

1. A. Beegom and M. Rajasree, A particle swarm optimization based pareto optimal task scheduling in cloud computing, in International Conference in Swarm Intelligence. Springer, 2014, pp. 79–86.
2. N. A. B. M. Shaari, T. F. Ang, L. Y. Por, and C. S. Liew, Dynamic pricing scheme for resource allocation in a multi-cloud environment, *Malaysian Journal of Computer Science*. 30(1) (2017), 1–11.
3. A. Liu and Z. Wang, Grid task scheduling based on adaptive ant colony algorithm, in International Conference on Management of e-Commerce and e-Government, 2008. ICMECG'08. IEEE, 2008, pp. 415–418.
4. C. Zhao, S. Zhang, Q. Liu, J. Xie, and J. Hu, Independent tasks scheduling based on the genetic algorithm in cloud computing, in 5th International Conference on Wireless Communications, Networking, and Mobile Computing, 2009. WiCom'09. IEEE, 2009, pp. 1–4.
5. A. Suresh and R. Varatharajan, Competent resource provisioning and distribution techniques for cloud computing environment, *Cluster Compututing*. (2017), 1–8.
6. B. Kruekaew and W. Kimpan, Virtual machine scheduling management on cloud computing using artificial bee colony, In Proceedings of the International MultiConference of engineers and computer scientists, 1 (2014), 1–5.

7. Jin X, Zhang F, Wang L, Hu S, Zhou B, and Liu Z, Joint optimization of operational cost and performance interference in cloud data centers, *IEEE Transactions on Cloud Computing*. 5(4) (Jun 25, 2015), 697–711.

8. J. Yu and R. Buyya, Scheduling scientific workflow applications with deadline and budget constraints using genetic algorithms, *Scientific Programming*. 14(3–4) (2006), 217–230.

9. S. G. Domanal and G. R. M. Reddy, An efficient cost optimized scheduling for spot instances in a heterogeneous cloud environment, *Future Generation Computer Systems*. 84 (2018), 11–21.

10. J. Gu, J. Hu, T. Zhao, and G. Sun, A new resource scheduling strategy based on a genetic algorithm in cloud computing environment, *Journal of Computers*. 7(1) (2012), 42–52.

11. Domanal SG and Reddy GR. Optimal load balancing in cloud computing by efficient utilization of virtual machines. In 2014 Sixth International Conference on Communication Systems and Networks (COMSNETS), Jan 6, 2014, pp. 1–4.

12. K. Kaur, A. Chhabra, and G. Singh, Heuristics based genetic algorithm for scheduling static tasks in the homogeneous parallel system, *International Journal of Computer Science and Security (IJCSS)*. 4(2) (2010), 183–198.

13. X. Lu and Z. Gu, A load-adaptive cloud resource scheduling model based on ant colony algorithm, in IEEE International Conference on Cloud Computing and Intelligence Systems (CCIS). IEEE, 2011, pp. 296–300.

14. J. J. Liang, A. K. Qin, P. N. Suganthan, and S. Baskar, Comprehensive learning particle swarm optimizer for global optimization of multimodal functions, *IEEE Transactions on Evolutionary Computation*. 10(3) (2006), 281–295.

15. M. Kalra and S. Singh, "A review of metaheuristic scheduling techniques in cloud computing," *Egyptian Informatics Journal*. 16(3), 275–295.

16. J. Fu, H. Zheng, and T. Mei, Look closer to see better: Recurrent attention convolutional neural network for fine-grained image recognition. In Proceedings of the IEEE conference on computer vision and pattern recognition, pp. 4438–4446. 2017.

17. Z. H. Zhan, X. F. Liu, Y. J. Gong, J. Zhang, H. S. H. Chung, and Y. Li, Cloud computing resource scheduling and a survey of its evolutionary approaches, *ACM Computing Surveys*. 47(4) (2015), 1–22.

18. Beloglazov A, Abawajy J and Buyya R, Energy-aware resource allocation heuristics for efficient management of data centers for cloud computing, *Future Generation Computer Systems*. 28(5) (May 1, 2012), 755–68.

19. Beheshti Z and Shamsuddin SM. A review of population-based meta-heuristic algorithms. *International Journal of Advances in Soft Computing and Its Application*. 5(1) (Mar. 1, 2013), 1–35.

20. T.A.L. Genez, L.F. Bittencourt, N.L.S. Da Fonseca, and E.R.M. Madeira, Estimation of the available bandwidth in inter-cloud links for task scheduling in hybrid clouds, *IEEE Transactions on Cloud Computing*. 7 (2019), pp. 62–74.

21. H.R. Faragardi, M.R. Saleh Sedghpour, S. Fazliahmadi, T. Fahringer, and N. Rasouli, GRP-HEFT: A budget-constrained resource provisioning scheme for workflow scheduling in IaaS clouds, *IEEE Transaction on Parallel Distributed System*. 31 (2020), pp. 1239–1254.

22. Q. Wu, M. Zhou, Q. Zhu, Y. Xia, and J. Wen, MOELS: Multiobjective evolutionary list scheduling for cloud workflows, *IEEE Transactions on Automation Science and Engineering*. 17 (2020), pp. 166–176.

23. V. Arabnejad, K. Bubendorfer, and B. Ng, Budget and deadline aware e-science workflow scheduling in clouds, *IEEE Transaction on Parallel Distributed System*. 30 (2019), pp. 29–44.

24. S.K. Mishra, D. Puthal, B. Sahoo, P.P. Jayaraman, S. Jun, A.Y. Zomaya, and R. Ranjan, Energy-efficient VM-placement in cloud data center, *Sustainable Computing: Informatics and Systems*. 20 (2018), pp. 48–55.

25. N. Mansouri, and M.M. Javidi, Cost-based job scheduling strategy in cloud computing environments, *Distributed Parallel Databases*. 38 (2020), pp. 365–400.

26. Y. Lu, and N. Sun, An effective task scheduling algorithm based on dynamic energy management and efficient resource utilization in green cloud computing environment, *Cluster Computing*. 22 (2019), pp. 513–520.

27. S. Sawant, A genetic algorithm scheduling approach for virtual machine resources in a cloud computing environment, Master's Theses, and Graduates Research, Paper 198, Master's Projects, San Jose State University, 2011.

28. P. Singh, P. Dimri, G. Saroha, and V. Barthwal, A load balancing analysis of cloud base application with different service broker policies, *IJCA*. 135(10) (2019), pp. 11–15.

29. M. Kalra and S. Singh, A review of meta heuristic scheduling techniques in cloud computing, *Egyptian Informatics Journal*. 3 (Jan. 2015), pp. 275–295.

30. A. Maas, A. Hannun, and A. Ng, Rectifier nonlinearities improve neural network acoustic models, in International Conference on Machine Learning (ICML), 2013.

31. S. Pang, W. Li, H. He, Z. Shan, and X. Wang, An EDA-GA hybrid algorithm for multi-objective task scheduling in cloud computing, *IEEE Access*. 7 (2019), pp.146379–146389.

CHAPTER 3

Neural Network-Based Resource Allocation Model in Multilayered Cloud

Rohit Verma and Punit Gupta

CONTENTS

DOI: 10.1201/9781003185376-3

3.1 INTRODUCTION

Cloud is basically a distributed computing environment which is scalable, pay-per-use and reliable. Cloud applications which are meant to provide computing in real-time require an efficient and cost-effective computing environment to provide a better cost-effective and reliable solution to the user. The resource allocation in a cloud computing environment depends on resources used, cost of resources and scheduler policy to improve the performance of the system. The local or global optimal point provides the solution [1, 2]. User requirements may be tested directly on a real cloud computing environment, but this increases the overhead costs; for example, Microsoft Azure and Amazon EC2 provide real test environments. The scalable simulation reduces the cost. Cloud computing provides dynamic services using virtual resources over the Internet [2]. The cloud service providers provide the facilities for the network, computing and storage as a service to the end-users. A. Liu et al. incorporate information from virtual computing environments and end-user experiences using an ant colony optimization approach [3].

Radojevic et al. suggested a threshold value for the connection time set between the client nodes. Resource provisioning techniques follow the features of the map between the virtual machine and a central resource monitor. Two attributes, bandwidth and delay, are used for the selection operator or cost-aware fitness value measurement. The nature-inspired biological technique follows a genetic approach that helps for the optimization of task allocation using selection operators. The genetic approach considers Big Bang (finite search space) having local optimal and optimal global solutions. The authors promulgated the throughput improvement and improved the power efficiency of the cloud using a meta-heuristic algorithm [4]. The authors do not focus on time and cost tradeoffs when the user requests increase.

The rapid elasticity features of the cloud handle multiple requests simultaneously. The elasticity policy includes automatic, reactive and active features of the scalable cloud computing environment [5]. The survey helps in service level agreement (SLA) management with resource availability and user satisfaction [6, 7]. The cost-aware technique is based on the optimization method Big Bang–Big Crunch using optimization criteria, task completion time and resource utilization cost. The heuristic-based approach supports an efficient resource allocation in a scalable cloud aura [8, 9]. The proposed model primarily focuses on performance improvement against the existing static, dynamic and meta-heuristic techniques [10–16]. The model aims to provide a cost-efficient solution to find a computing resource which can complete the task with least execution time and least cost to compute the data of real-time application in the most efficient manner and provide better QoS to the users.

3.2 RELATED WORK

Cloud computing is an upcoming technology in many forms. In this section a study of task scheduling is showcased. This technology is still growing in which the computing paradigm encapsulates the application software in a virtual machine and data centers. In the real world cloud is a heterogeneous combination of various services providers providing various storage, networking and processing services to the user on pay-per-use model. Cloud computing is responsible for executing the user task with high computation and least cost as promised to the user without compromising on either quality matrices. To manage this task, scheduling plays an important role in improving the performance of the cloud and quality of service for users. The dynamic scheduling algorithm provides a better quality of service than the static scheduling techniques [17]. The prominent benefits of scheduling algorithms are to achieve high-performance computing and optimal system throughput. X. Jin et al. proclaimed a general technique that captures the tradeoff between time and cost [18].

The tasks are mapped on a central processing unit on a priority basis. It depends on the burst time of the tasks. Domanal et al. [19] exhibited the load balancer policy in a static environment. The quality of service is measured using the average response time. Still, there is scope for the efficient allocation of the virtual machine using meta-heuristic techniques [20]. S.G. Damanal et al. [21] revealed the status of the virtual machines in a cloud computing environment. The authors have also considered the active load balancer as the key focus area of the work. There is scope to implement the policy which supports the dynamic environment and scalable simulation. Researchers described the load balancing scheme for the private cloud. The performance measurement criteria include utilization standards. The authors primarily focused on bio-inspired meta-heuristic techniques for the performance measurement of the scalable cloud [22]. The authors have proposed an act colony-based nature-inspired algorithm and particle swarm model to improve the performance of cloud resource allocation [23, 24]. Kalra et al. provided the detailed survey on first come first serve (FCFS), local search algorithm, stochastic hill climbing (SHC) and soft computing approaches with the genetic algorithm (GA) [17, 25–27]. The authors also presented the various optimization criteria for the optimal global solution.

The authors primarily focused on task mapping on virtual machines. The quality of service improves further using multiple performance measurement parameters. N. Panwar et al. focused on task scheduling in a scalable cloud computing environment. The authors focused on a hybrid approach. The hybrid approach is known as the TOPSIS-PSO technique. The performance is measured in terms of makespan and cost of the resources. The results are generated using only fabricated datasets. P.Y. Zhang and M.C. Zhou focused on a two-stage scheduling strategy. The proposed strategy is compared against broadly adopted techniques in cloud computing, i.e., max-min and min-min task scheduling techniques [28]. Z.H. Zhan et al. [29] focused on a comprehensive survey of state-of-the-art approaches used in resource provisioning. This hybrid approach is compared with the modified cost-aware BB–BC and bio-inspired intelligence systems. The bio-inspired intelligence systems neural-GA and neural-BB–BC-cost-aware techniques improve performance metrics.

Singh et al. has proposed a model for task allocation for cloud. The BB–BC-cost model is used to improve resource allocation [30]. Wei et al. proposed a heterogeneous resource allocation approach for multi-resource allocation. The multi-resource allocation includes virtual machine allocation [31]. Wu et al. proposed a multi-objective evolutionary list scheduling approach using performance metrics cost and makespan [32]. Most of the above-discussed work can be categorized as algorithms to improve cost and time, but no algorithm exists which tries to improve both parameters at the same time. Therefore this work aims to improve both performance parameters together to provide the least cost to the client and manage high performance at the cloud infrastructure end.

Table 3.1 provides a comparative study of existing techniques for task scheduling for the cloud [36–42]. The comparison has categorized the algorithm based on the performance parameter taken into consideration by the existing approaches, i.e., cost, execution time, utilization and power consumption. It has been found that most of the work focuses on only one parameter at a time but the efficiency cannot be achieved if all parameters are taken into consideration. The above-discussed comparative study

TABLE 3.1 Comparative Study of Existing Work

Reference	Strategy	Type	Performance Metrics			
			Cost	Makespan/Execution Time	Utilization	Power
[2]	Ant colony	Task scheduling	-	Yes	-	-
[3]	Genetic algorithm	Task scheduling	-	Yes	-	-
[33]	OCRP algorithm	Task scheduling	Yes	-	-	-
[11]	Artificial bee colony	VM scheduling	-	Yes	-	-
[12]	Multi-objective	Task scheduling	Yes	-	-	-
[14]	Genetic algorithm	Task scheduling	-	Yes	-	Yes
[15]	Genetic algorithm	Task scheduling	-	Yes	-	-
[34]	Ant colony	Task scheduling	-	Yes	Yes	-
[4]	Evolutionary technique	Task scheduling	-	-	Yes	Yes
[6]	Iterative ordinal optimization (IOO)	Workflow scheduling	-	Yes	Yes	-
[8]	Particle swarm optimization (PSO)	Task scheduling	Yes	-	-	-
[9]	Big Bang theory	Task scheduling	-	Yes	-	-
[18]	Minimum increasing cost algorithm (MIC)	VM scheduling	Yes	Yes	-	-
[35]	Genetic algorithm	Workflow scheduling	Yes	-	-	-
[19]	Artificial neural network	Task scheduling	Yes	Yes	Yes	-
[20]	Genetic algorithm	Task scheduling	-	Yes	-	-
[21]	Evolutionary technique	Load balancing	-	Yes	-	-
[24]	Particle swarm optimization (PSO)	Task scheduling	-	Yes	-	-
[35]	Evolutionary technique	Task scheduling	Yes	-	-	-
[36]	Evolutionary technique	Task scheduling	Yes	Yes	-	-

showcases the importance of various performance parameters and a need for a multi-objective optimization algorithm for task scheduling in the cloud to improve cost, execution time and utilization at the same time. This work aims to overcome the disadvantages of existing approaches and provide a global best solution to improve the quality of service of the cloud.

3.3 PROPOSED MODEL

This section showcases the proposed algorithm for task allocation for cloud infrastructure. The novelty of the proposed BB–BC ANN cost-aware technique is to increase the execution time, cost and convergence rate. It provides an optimal global solution with a fast convergence rate which provides a cost-efficient solution for the client. To overcome the drawbacks of existing cost-aware scheduling algorithms, a cost-aware BB–BC ANN algorithm is proposed. The proposed cost-aware BB–BC ANN technique is based on the theory of the universe in astronomy. The proposed cost-efficient Big Bang–Big Crunch task scheduling approach is inspired by a hypothesis of evaluation of the universe, according to which the universe started with the Big Bang and spread into parts that are attracted by a single force toward a single point black hole. In the second phase, the strong and healthy part combines with the removal of unhealthy parts and the universe will combine at a single point with one stable universe. The proposed algorithm considers that a cloud is a heterogeneous combination of various service providers which provide services with varying cost, resources and performance. Cloud controller and task scheduling policy is responsible for finding a suitable resource on a service provider to complete the task in the least time, execution cost and with a defined quality of service. The proposed algorithm is meant to cover all the performance parameters discussed above.

The proposed algorithm is divided into two parts: trained model preparation and prediction. The training model preparation phase is divided into the below listed phases:

1. Model setup.

2. Dataset generation.

3. Model designing.

4. Training.

5. Backpropagation.

6. Task allocation.

3.3.1 Model Setup

In this phase the initialization of basic parameters for the trained model is done where the count of neurons in the input layer, output layer and hidden layer are defined along with the number of hidden layers and lastly the activation function.

Along with this the input parameters for BB–BC are also defined including population size, mutation rate and learning rate. This module defines the scalability and accuracy of the trained model.

3.3.2 Dataset Generation

In this module the dataset for model training and testing is generated using the proposed model. This module defines the accuracy of the model to predict the best global solution with the least cost and execution time.

The proposed BB–BC algorithm for generating a dataset with a defined cost-aware fitness function is defined in Section 3.3.7. The input to the proposed model in the configuration of the resources and task. Where resources refer to the host and virtual machine configuration with cost and resources available.

The algorithm is designed to find a global optimum solution in the least number of evolutions and mutations. The proposed model takes care of both cost and utilization of the resources to improve the power consumption of the system.

$$\text{fitness value}_i = \sum_{j=1}^{j=n} \alpha * \text{cost}_j + \beta * \text{task completion\_time}_j \qquad (3.1)$$

Where $\alpha + \beta = 1$.

$$\text{Total\_Execution\_time} = \sum_{i=1}^{n} \text{Task\_Length}_i / \text{MIPS}_j \qquad (3.2)$$

Equation 3.1 defines the fitness function which is the summation of computational cost and the execution time in a proportion defined by α and β, where the sum of α and β is 1.

3.3.3 Model Preparation

In this phase the artificial neural network (ANN) is defined using the parameters defined in the setup phase. The model takes input as the number of neurons in the input, output and hidden layers. The model also takes the number of hidden layers as input. The activation function is used to initialize and adjust the weight of a neuron and is also responsible for adjusting the further weights during error propagation. The activation function at the input layer is a sigmoidal function.

The proposed ANN model uses a feedforward network and backpropagation for adjusting weight to fit the model to the target dataset. The accuracy of the ANN model depends on the type of data, number of hidden layers and number of neurons. The higher the dependency between the dataset the larger the number of hidden layers and neurons required.

3.3.4 Training

In the training phase, the dataset generated in phase 2 is divided into two parts, i.e., a training dataset and a testing dataset in a ratio of 80/20%, where 80% of data is used for training the model and 20% of data is used for testing and error propagation to improve the accuracy of model iteration by integration. This phase defines the accuracy of the model by adjusting the weights of the neurons in each iteration.

The process of training aims to get the minimum fitness value defined and set the weight accordingly. The training dataset generated by the proposed BB–BC algorithm aims to find least cost and execution time at the same time, which is used to trained the ANN model.

The activation function Leaky ReLU is used at hidden layers and the sigmoidal function is used at the output layer. The activation function plays an important role in dataset training which defines the accuracy to model fitting.

3.3.5 Backpropagation and Error Correction

Here the objective of this phase is to improve the accuracy of the neural network by adjusting the weights of the neurons at the input layer and hidden layer to achieve the desired output. This phase plays an important role in weight adjustment to make the model more accurate and predict the value more accurately. This process improves the gap between the expected value and the actual value; in our case it is finding the resource with least cost and execution time.

$$e_k(n) = d_k(n) - y_k(n) \qquad (3.3)$$

$$\delta_k = \frac{1}{2} * e_k^2(n) \qquad (3.4)$$

In Equation 3.3 and Equation 3.4, the parameter $d_k(n)$ denotes the expected output, $y_k(n)$ denotes the exact output and $e_k(n)$ is the error, and δ_k is the cost function used in the learning process of the ANN model respectively.

3.3.6 Task Scheduling

In this phase, the perceptron model with appropriate training is used for task scheduling to reduce the scheduling time, power efficiency, cost and total execution time of the tasks.

3.3.7 Steps of Big Bang–Big Crunch

The proposed algorithm considers that a cloud is a heterogeneous combination of various services providers which provide services with varying cost, resources and performance. Cloud controller and task scheduling policy is responsible for finding a suitable resource on a service provider to complete the task in the least time and execution cost and with a defined quality of service. The proposed algorithm is meant to cover all the performance parameters discussed above.

The proposed algorithm is divided into seven modules:

Module 1: Initialization.

Module 2: Evaluation.

Module 3: Selection.

Module 4: Crossover.

Module 5: Mutation.

Module 6: Big crunch/optimization of task allocation on virtual machines.

Module 7: Stopping condition.

3.3.7.1 Initialization

In this phase all the parameters required are initialized as shown in Table 3.2. The input of the algorithms is defined in this phase.

3.3.7.2 Evaluation

In this phase, the fitness value for each schedule has generated the schedule is also named as one population. Fitness plays an important role in

TABLE 3.2 Input Parameters Used in the Proposed Technique

Hyper parameters	Hidden layer: 1, hidden units = 3, learning rate = 0.2
Mutation rate	0.15
Evolution	100
Population size	100
Number of hidden layers	4
Neurons in output layer	50/100
Neurons in each hidden layer	50
Activation function	*Leaky* Relue *Activation* function = $f(x) =$ $\{\alpha * x \text{ if } x \leq 0, x \text{ if } x > 0\}$ $\forall \alpha = 0.01$

identifying whether the schedule will take part in the next generation of evolution or not. Fitness in BB–BC is also referred to as the mass of the schedule. In the proposed algorithm the fitness function is defined as fol-lows: Fitness value$_i$ is defined as the fitness of ith population, where the fitness function is the sum of cost and execution of each task over a VM where j states the number of tasks and $\alpha + \beta = 1$.

$$\text{fitness value}_i = \sum_{j=1}^{j=n} \alpha * \cos t_j + \beta * \text{task completion\_time}_j \quad (3.6)$$

The task completion time variable is measured using Equation 3.7 in which Task_Length is the number of instructions in a task, *VM_MIPS* is the MIPS of VM and *PE* is the processor count.

$$\text{task\_completion\_time}_i = \frac{\text{Task\_Length}_i}{\text{VM\_MIPS}_i \times PE_i} \quad (3.7)$$

$$\cos t_i = \text{Network\_delay}_i + \text{task\_completion\_time}_i$$
$$\times ((\text{ram\_size} \times \cos t \, \text{PerRam}) + (\text{mips} \times \cos t \, \text{Per Mips}) \quad (3.8)$$
$$+ (\text{Number Of Pes} \times \cos t \, \text{Per Second}) + (bw \times \cos t \, \text{Per } Bw))$$

Equation 3.8 defines the cost of resources used during the execution of a task at a specific VM.

In this phase the mass of all the schedules is evaluated using the fitness function shown in Equation 3.2. Evolution is a set of steps repeated in every evolution which include selection, crossover, mutation and the big crunch phase. The fitness function proposed is a multi-objective function for cost and execution time which the intern improves the utilization of the system.

3.3.7.3 Selection

In this phase two best solutions are selected. The first solution is the one with the least cost and the second solution is the one with fitness value near to the center of mass of all the solutions which means the solution with fitness value nearest to the center of mass. The center of mass or contraction operator is calculated using Equation 3.9. The center of mass is denoted by x^c. Its values are calculated using the formula below:

$$ x^c = \frac{\sum_{i=1}^{i=N} \frac{1}{f_i} x_i}{\sum_{i=1}^{i=N} \frac{1}{f_i}} \tag{3.9}$$

The second-best solution is the solution near the center of mass. The two solutions take part in the next evolution which includes crossover and mutation to improve the next generation and find the next best solution in the solution space.

3.3.7.4 Crossover

This phase takes two best solutions from the selection phase as input, and a multi-point crossover is performed in which the swapping of a random point between two solutions selected is done. This phase aims to design a better offspring solution using two input solutions from the selection phase.

3.3.7.5 Mutation

In this phase, the third-best solution discovered spreads its diversity in other populations using swapping-based mutation of the candidate solution in a search space with other solutions. The swapping is performed with a low mutation rate which helps to retail the core features of the chromosome. This step resembles a biological mutation in the real world.

3.3.7.6 Big Crunch

This phase plays an important role in improving the performance and increasing the probability of finding the best solution by reducing the search space in each evaluation until one element remains. This step first finds the one worst solution with the highest fitness value from the evaluation phase. The solution with the worst fitness solution is removed from the population. This phase reduces the number of solutions in each evaluation which resembles the big crunch phase of the algorithm which says that only the fittest will survive in the evolutions and the worst will be left out. This reduction will reduce the time consumed in the evaluation and selection phase with upcoming evolutions.

3.3.7.7 Stopping Condition

The stopping condition for the proposed algorithm is the number of evolutions and number of solutions left, whichever reaches one first, or else repeat phases 3.2, 3.3, 3.4, 3.5 and 3.6 until one best solution is left or the number of evolutions is completed. This condition defines that if the size of populations is very large in that case number of evolution is the stopping condition else if the population reached one, i.e., only one solution is left which is considered the best solution. Figures 3.1 and 3.2 showcase the model and flow diagram for the proposed algorithm.

Table 3.2 shows all the parameters taken into consideration for the proposed algorithm.

3.3.8 Results and Discussions

Simulation is performed using Cloudsim 3.0. The simulation uses workload traces for real-time task simulation which is a SWF format workload file from parallel workload, a free open-source dataset from parallel workload repository.

In this section, the performance evaluation of the proposed model is carried out. Many criteria are used for task scheduling evaluation. Many of the metrics are given below:

- Total execution time (millisecond).

- Average finish time (millisecond).

- Cost ($).

- Network delay (millisecond).

- Power consumption (kWh).

Figures 3.3 and 3.4 show a comparative study for 200 tasks with 10 virtual machines, 3 data centers and increasing population size in order to find a

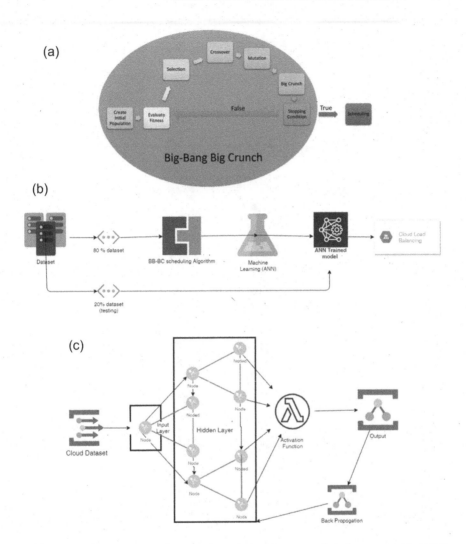

FIGURE 3.1   (a) Proposed BB–BC algorithm. (b) Proposed architecture. (c) ANN proposed.

better solution. This figure compares the proposed algorithm with existing cost-aware genetic algorithms and genetic algorithms with execution time as a fitness function. This experiment shows that with the increasing size of the population the probability of finding a better solution increases; when compared to existing algorithms the proposed model results in the least total execution time and average finish time. Figure 3.4 shows a comparative study of execution time for 200 tasks with increasing population size where the number of VMs and data centers remains the same. Here average finish time and execution time are taken as performance

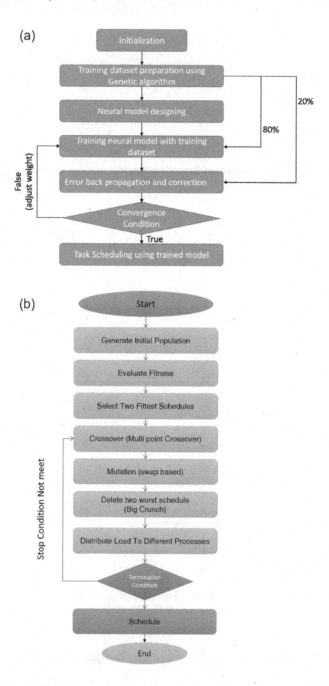

FIGURE 3.2 (a) Flowchart of proposed task allocation technique. (b) Flowchart of BB–BC algorithm.

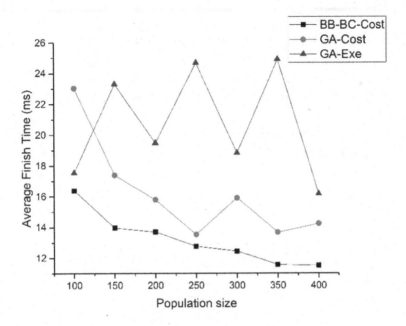

FIGURE 3.3   Study of average finish time vs population size.

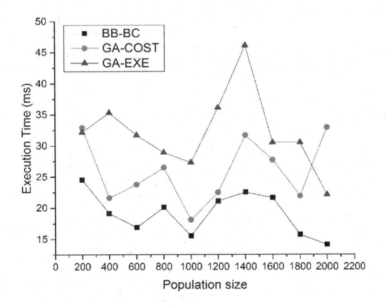

FIGURE 3.4   Study of average execution time vs population size.

parameters to evaluate the time performance of the proposed algorithm. Figure 3.5 shows a comparative study of average finish time for increasing load, i.e., the number of tasks keeping resources a constant.

This experiment is performed to study the impact of load, i.e., increasing number of tasks on finish time and execution time in underloaded and overloaded conditions. The results show that the proposed algorithm. Figure 3.6 shows a comparative study of the execution cost of resources with an increasing number of tasks where the proposed model outperforms the existing work with three VMs. This study showcases the improvement in finish time and execution time in the underloaded and overloaded conditions in which the proposed algorithm proves to outperform the existing algorithms.

Figures 3.7 and 3.8 show the same comparative study with cost as a performance metric with ten VMs to study the behavior of the proposed algorithm under overloaded and underloaded conditions. The proposed algorithm performs better in both scenarios. Figure 3.8 shows a comparative study over average cost as a performance matrix to study the performance of the proposed algorithm with increasing population size, i.e., the search space for the algorithm. The proposed algorithm proves to be better than the existing model. Figure 3.9 shows the comparative study of

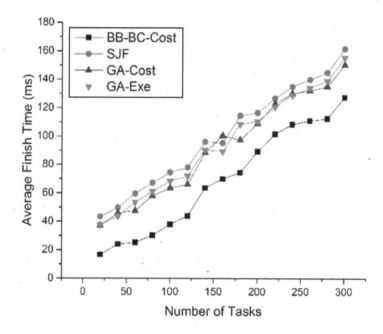

FIGURE 3.5   Study of average finish time vs number of tasks.

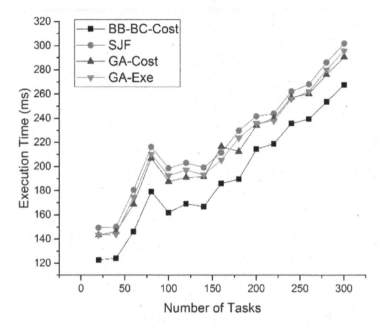

FIGURE 3.6   Study of execution cost vs tasks for three virtual machines.

network delay as a performance parameter since the proposed algorithm takes into consideration network delay. The proposed algorithm performs better than existing models in reducing the network delay since total execution time is the sum of waiting time, network delay and execution time. Most of the existing work considers execution time which is an incomplete performance matrix. Figure 3.10 shows a comparison of power consumed by an existing algorithm and proposed bio-inspired algorithms. The proposed algorithm outperforms the time-aware and cost-aware bio-inspired genetic technique. The performance of the genetic approach is improved by using the BB–BC, which is embedded inside the bio-inspired approach.

3.4 CONCLUSION AND FUTURE WORKS

In this paper, an efficient task scheduling scheme was presented for task scheduling in cloud infrastructure. The projected model outperforms the genetic approach and existing techniques. The results section shows that the projected model performs better than the existing techniques for cloud IAAS. The results are compared using finish time, start time and cost as performance matrix in this work focused only on task scheduling in cloud using a BB–BC algorithm. The work has proposed a model with high quality of service. In future work, the proposed model will be used for resource scheduling on host

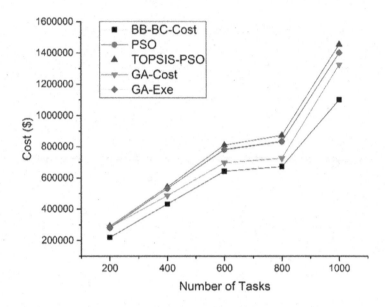

FIGURE 3.7   Study of execution cost vs number of tasks for ten virtual machines.

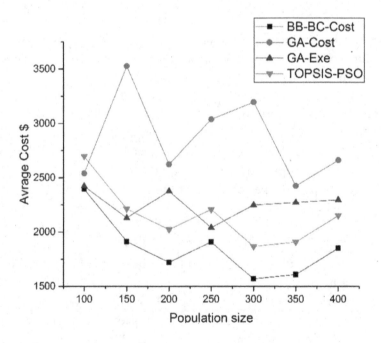

FIGURE 3.8   Study of execution cost vs populations size.

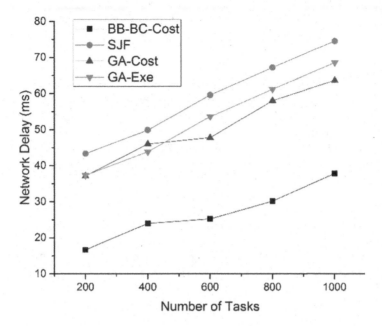

FIGURE 3.9   Study of network delay vs number of tasks.

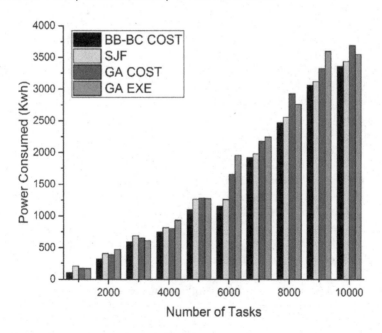

FIGURE 3.10   Study of power consumed vs number of tasks.

and migration approaches for better utilization of resources to improve the running cost of cloud applications with optimal resources.

REFERENCES

1. M Rajasree and A A Beegom, "A particle swarm optimization based pareto optimal task scheduling in cloud computing," in International Conference in Swarm Intelligence. Springer, 2014, pp.79–86.
2. NABM Shaari, LY Por, TF Ang, and CS Liew, "Dynamic pricing scheme for resource allocation in a multi-cloud environment," *Malaysian J. Comput. Sci.*, 2017, vol. 30(1), pp. 1–11.
3. Z Wang and A Liu, "Grid task scheduling based on adaptive ant colony algorithm," in International Conference on Management of e-Commerce and e-Government, 2008. ICMECG'08. IEEE, 2008, pp. 415–418.
4. Sheikh HF, Fan D., and Ahmad I, "An evolutionary technique for performance-energy-temperature optimized scheduling of parallel tasks on multi-core processors," *IEEE Transactions on Parallel and Distributed Systems*, 2015 Apr 9, vol. 27(3), pp. 668–81.
5. Mladenow A., Strauss C., and Kryvinska N, "Towards cloud-centric service environments," *Journal of Service Science Research*, 2012 Dec 1, vol.4(2), pp. 213–234.
6. Zhang F, Hwang K, Cao J, Li K, and Khan SU, "Adaptive workflow scheduling on cloud computing platforms with iterative ordinal optimization," *IEEE Transactions on Cloud Computing*, 2014 Aug 21, 3(2), pp. 156–68.
7. Venticinque S, Di Martino B, Aversa R, Rak M, and Petcu D, "A cloud agency for SLA negotiation and management," in European Conference on Parallel Processing, 2010 Aug 31, pp. 587–594.
8. Guo L, Zhao S, Shen S, and Jiang C, "Task scheduling optimization in cloud computing based on heuristic algorithm," *Journal of Networks*, 2012 Mar 1, vol. 7(3), pp. 547–567.
9. Rawat PS, Saroha GP, and Dimri P, "Virtual machine allocation to the task using an optimization method in cloud computing environment," *International Journal of Information Technology*, 2018, pp. 1–9.
10. A Suresh and R Varatharajan, "Competent resource provisioning and distribution techniques for cloud computing environment," *Cluster Computing*, 2017, pp. 1–8.
11. B Kruekaew and W Kimpan, "Virtual machine scheduling management on cloud computing using artificial bee colony," 2014, vol. 1, pp. 1–5.
12. Craciun C and Frincu ME, "Multi-objective meta-heuristics for scheduling applications with high availability requirements and cost constraints in multi-cloud environments," in 2011 Fourth IEEE International Conference on Utility and Cloud Computing, 2011 Dec 5, pp. 267–274.
13. Wickremasinghe B, Buyya R, and Calheiros RN, "Cloudanalyst: A cloud-sim-based visual modeler for analyzing cloud computing environments and applications," in 2010 24th IEEE International Conference on Advanced Information Networking and Applications, 2010 Apr 20, pp. 446–452.

14. K Chandrasekaran, CT Joseph, and R Cyriac, "A novel family genetic approach for virtual machine allocation," *Procedia Computer Science*, 2014, vol. 46(Icict), pp. 558–565.
15. Zhang S, Zhao C, Liu Q, Xie J, and Hu J, "Independent tasks scheduling based on genetic algorithm in cloud computing," in 2009 5th International Conference on Wireless Communications, Networking and Mobile Computing, 2009 Sep 24, pp. 1–4.
16. P Rawat, "A survey and analysis with different resource provisioning strategies in cloud environment," vol. 1, pp. 339–345.
17. M Kalra and S Singh, "A review of metaheuristic scheduling techniques in cloud computing," *Egyptian Informatics Journal*, vol. 16(3), pp. 275–295.
18. Jin X, Zhang F, Hu S, Zhou B, Wang L, and Liu Z, "Joint optimization of operational cost and performance interference in cloud data centers," *IEEE Transactions on Cloud Computing*, 2015 Jun 25, vol. 5(4), pp. 697–711.
19. SG Domanal and GRM Reddy, "An efficient cost optimized scheduling for spot instances in a heterogeneous cloud environment," *Future Generation Computer Systems*, vol. 84, pp. 2018.
20. J Gu, J Hu, T Zhao, and G Sun, "A new resource scheduling strategy based on a genetic algorithm in cloud computing environment," *Journal of Computers*, 2012, vol. 7(1), pp. 42–52.
21. Reddy GR, and Domanal SG, Optimal load balancing in cloud computing by efficient utilization of virtual machines. In 2014 Sixth International Conference on Communication Systems and Networks (COMSNETS), 2014 Jan 6, pp. 1–4.
22. K Kaur, G Singh, and A Chhabra, "Heuristics based genetic algorithm for scheduling static tasks in the homogeneous parallel system," *International Journal of Computer Science and Security*, 2010, vol. 4(2), pp. 183–198.
23. X Lu and Z Gu, "A load-adaptive cloud resource scheduling model based on ant colony algorithm," in 2011 IEEE International Conference on Cloud Computing and Intelligence Systems. IEEE, 2011, pp. 296–300.
24. JJ Liang, AK Qin, PN Suganthan, and S Baskar, "Comprehensive learning particle swarm optimizer for global optimization of multimodal functions," *IEEE Transactions on Evolutionary Computation*, 2006, vol. 10(3), pp. 281–295.
25. Beloglazov A, Buyya R, and Abawajy J, "Energy-aware resource allocation heuristics for efficient management of data centers for cloud computing," *Future Generation Computer Systems*, 2012 May 1, vol 28(5), pp. 755–68.
26. Beheshti Z and Shamsuddin SM, A review of population-based meta-heuristic algorithms. *International Journal of Advances in Soft Computing and Its Application*, 2013 Mar 1, vol. 5(1), pp. 1–35.
27. MA Rodriguez and R Buyya, "Scheduling algorithm for scientific workflows on clouds," 2014, vol. 2(2), pp. 222–235.
28. PY Zhang and MC Zhou, "Dynamic cloud task scheduling based on a two-stage strategy," *IEEE Transactions on Automation Science and Engineering*, 2018, 15(2), pp. 772–783.

29. ZH Zhan, YJ Gong XF Liu, J Zhang, HSH Chung, and Y Li, "Cloud computing resource scheduling and a survey of its evolutionary approaches," *ACM Computing Surveys*, 2015, 47(4), pp. 1–22.

30. Rawat, PS, Dimri, P, Kanrar, S, and Saroha, GP, "Optimize task allocation in cloud environment based on big-bang big-crunch. *Wireless Personal Communications*, pp. 1–44.

31. Wei, L, Foh, CH, He, B, and Cai, J, "Towards efficient resource allocation for heterogeneous workloads in IaaS clouds," *IEEE Transactions on Cloud Computing*, 2018, vol. 6(1), pp. 264–275.

32. Wu, Q, Zhou, M, Zhu, Q, Xia, Y, and Wen, J, "MOELS: Multiobjective evolutionary list scheduling for cloud workflows," *IEEE Transactions on Automation Science and Engineering*, 2020, vol. 17(1), pp. 166–176.

33. C Zhao, Q Liu, J Xie, S Zhang, and J Hu, "Independent tasks scheduling based on the genetic algorithm in cloud computing," in 5th International Conference on Wireless Communications, Networking, and Mobile Computing, 2009. WiCom'09. IEEE, 2009, pp. 1–4.

34. Y-C Lee, C-W Chiang, C-N Lee, and T-Y Chou, "Ant colony optimization for task matching and scheduling," *IEE Proceedings-Computers and Digital Techniques*, vol. 153(6), pp. 373–380.

35. J Yu and R Buyya, "Scheduling scientific workflow applications with deadline and budget constraints using genetic algorithms," *Scientific Programming*, vol. 14(4), pp. 217–230.

36. Kumar BA and Ravichandran T, "Time and cost optimization algorithm for scheduling multiple workflows in hybrid clouds," *European Journal of Scientific Research*, 2012 Oct, vol. 89(2), pp. 265–75.

37. DC Devi and VR Uthariaraj, "Load balancing in cloud computing environment using improved weighted round robin algorithm for nonpreemptive dependent tasks," 2016, vol. 2016, pp. 1–8.

38. SHH Madni, Y Coulibaly, MSA Latiff, and SM Abdulhamid, "Recent advancements in resource allocation techniques for cloud computing environment: a systematic review," *Cluster Computing*, 2017, vol. 20(3), pp. 2489–2533.

39. OK Erol and I Eksin, "A new optimization method: Big Bang-Big Crunch," *Advances in Engineering Software*, 2006, vol. 37(2), pp. 106–111.

40. GM Jaradat and M Ayob, "Big Bang-Big Crunch optimization algorithm to solve the course timetabling problem," in Proceedings of the 2010 10th International Conference Intelligent Systems Des. Appl. ISDA', 2010, vol. 10, pp. 1448–1452.

41. Firdhous M, Hassan S., and Ghazali O, "Modeling of cloud system using Erlang formulas," in The 17th Asia Pacific Conference on Communications, 2011 Oct 2, pp. 411–416.

42. Zhang Y, Wang X, and Wang Y, "Greenware: Greening cloud-scale data centers to maximize the use of renewable energy," in ACM/IFIP/USENIX International Conference on Distributed Systems Platforms and Open Distributed Processing, 2011 Dec 12, pp. 143–164.

CHAPTER 4

Consideration of Availability and Reliability in Cloud Computing

Dheeraj Rane, Vaishali Chourey,
Rohit Verma and Punit Gupta

CONTENTS

4.1 INTRODUCTION

The aim of this work is to propose a systematic description of the parameters availability and reliability that define cloud computing QoS. Compliance with the minimum service standard can be verified competently using these formal concepts. This is the first step in a long process of developing a complete blueprint for cloud Service Level Agreement (SLA) and the mathematical understanding that determines the successful use of SLA in monitoring the cloud services and ensuring QoS.

DOI: 10.1201/9781003185376-4

WS-Agreement Andrieux [1], Web Service Level Agreement (WSLA) Keller [2], SLAng Lamanna [3] and Web Service Offering Language Tosic [4] are a few well-known SLA structures for web services (WSOL). The terminology used for implementation, the conditions considered, the way restrictions are applied and the adapted life cycle are all different. Since both web services and cloud computing are built on a service-oriented architecture, they have a lot in common when it comes to SLAs. However, due to the variety of cloud computing service implementation models (e.g., SaaS, PaaS and IaaS), many additional criteria must be considered [5–10]. This chapter is organized as follows: The next section sets the platform by proving the need for SLA and importance of availability and reliability in cloud computing. Section 4.2 details the related work about SLA, availability and reliability in cloud computing. Clear definitions of availability and reliability are provided in Section 4.3. Section 4.4 summarizes the chapter.

There are lots of SLA templates for technologies with concepts similar to those of cloud computing such as web services, grid and utility computing. The majority of the templates of related technologies are either specific to those technologies, are under development or several features of the SLA life cycle that would be required for the cloud. Indeed, these SLA templates cannot be adopted in their original form in the context of cloud computing. Table 4.1 gives a comparison of three technologies [10–15], namely cloud computing, Grid computing and Web services. This contrast reveals that the services offered by web services and those provided by the cloud are vastly different. A web service is an application that exposes a function accessible using standard web technologies and that adheres to web services standards. This means web service is only a small concept within one of the service models (2010) of cloud computing known as SaaS. In a similar manner, differences exist between grid computing and the cloud as well. These differences are mainly related to service models, multi-level SLA, virtual organization, task size, scalability and more. As a result, current SLA models can't handle the variety of cloud applications. Furthermore, they are constrained to QoS, specifically cost and performance analysis, and do not consider several non-functional issues such as risk, trust or green computing. All of this adds to the need for a cloud computing-specific SLA template.

4.2 RELATED WORK

Cloud computing may be thought of as a continuation of the web services and their concepts [16]. Grid computing [11] can also be considered an

TABLE 4.1   Comparison of Cloud Computing, Grid Computing and Web Services

Consideration	Cloud Computing	Grid Computing	Web Services
Computing	Standalone or Parallel	Parallel	Standalone
Type of service	SaaS, PaaS and IaaS	Usually infrastructure	B2B Service
SLA	Yes	Limited	Yes
Multi-level SLA	Yes	No	No
Protocols	TCP/IP, SOAP, REST	MPI, MPI-CHG, GIS, GRAM	SOAP, REST
Virtualization	Yes	Limited	No
Virtual Organization	No	Yes	No
Interoperability	Limited	Yes	Yes
Different service Models	Yes	Mostly related to infrastructure needs	Mostly B2B, end user is not involved
Resource Handling	Centralized as well as Distributed	Distributed	Centralized
Task size	Depends on service models. Varies from small to large	Single large	Small
Scalable	Full	Limited	No
Multi-tenancy	Yes	Yes	No
Application	SME and interactive applications	HPC	Limited to B2B for data retrieval
Standardization	No	Yes	Yes
Software Dependency	Independent	Application domain dependent software	Independent
Platform	Service model Dependent	Grid compliant software is must	Independent
Operating System	Hypervisor running multiple OS	Standard OS	Standard OS
Failure Management	Strong (VMs can be migrated)	Limited	Limited
User friendliness	High	Low	As B2B, so no interaction with end user
Security	Required	Required only from non-users	Almost secure

intellectual cousin of cloud computing, with utility computing serving as its foundation [17]. As a result, we divide the literature review on the SLA template into three categories: (a) grid SLA, (b) web services SLA and (c) utility computing SLA. Since cloud-related SLA problems are still emerging, the context could include SLA for grids and service-oriented architecture (SOA). Following is a survey of current SLA frameworks [18], accompanied by a discussion on the scope of defining new SLA in cloud scenarios.

The Open Grid Forum [19] described WS-Agreement, a language and protocol for advertising service providers' capabilities, creating agreements based on templates and tracking agreement enforcement at run-time. It improves on traditional service discovery and usage models such as Universal Description, Discovery and Integration (UDDI), since it enables service users to discover available services, to use services and to dynamically negotiate the service's efficiency. Initially, there was no negotiation process, but now WS-Agreement can be addressed in all five stages of the SLA life cycle. It should be noted that the scope of the project is limited to web services and grid computing only.

Web Service Level Agreement (WSLA) is a system established by Keller et al. in 2003 [2] for defining and tracking service level agreements for web services. The WSLA framework includes a scalable and extensible language based on the XML schema, as well as a run-time architecture that includes many SLA monitoring services that can be outsourced to third parties for full objectivity. Customers and providers can use WSLA to identify a broad range of SLAs, determine SLA parameters and how they're calculated and link them to controlled resource instrumentation. The WSLA monitoring services are automatically configured to implement the SLA once an SLA specification is received. WSLA has a lot of versatility when it comes to defining inter- and intra-organizational SLA parameters to XML. It does not, however, have multi-level SLA.

A language (SLAng) was proposed by Lamanna [3] for generating SLA for the application service provision scenario, in which a client submits a request to a service, which processes the request and returns a response to the network. Specifications are divided into two groups by SLAng: generic and ASP standards. The SLAng semantics are defined using the Essential Meta-Object Facility (EMOF), a modeling language similar to UML. Models help to make QoS parameters more understandable. The presence of SLA elements also restricts the types of behaviors that can be found in the model. Object Constraint Language is used to define constraints in SLAng (OCL). While SLA has the advantage of being implemented using a modeling language, it cannot be used in practice since it is still in progress, is not appropriate for multi-level SLA and only considers a few parameters.

Wu et al. in 2010 presented an SLA management system for utility computing services. The SLA management architecture is made up of layers that analyze and verify the allocation of resources.

The project SLA@SOI [8] envisions a business-ready service-oriented infrastructure and has created an SLA-enabled reference architecture which can be used to support new and existing service-oriented cloud infrastructures. SLA* is a project that is developing a language that provides domain-independent syntax for machine readable SLAs. SLA* is a service level agreement that applies to all facilities, not just those provided by technology. It is also language agnostic.

A method for adaptive SLA template generation was proposed by Brandic et al. [20]. As a result, a method of SLA management is provided, allowing gaps between two SLAs to be removed and mapping rules to be specified. When service consumers reach providers dynamically and on demand, this will be useful. They do not, however, suggest mapping tracked metrics to agreed-upon SLAs.

4.3 AVAILABILITY AND RELIABILITY IN CLOUD SLA

SLAs implemented by technologies similar to cloud computing cannot be explicitly used for the same in their original form due to variations in their underlying implementation. The features and parameters that must be present in a cloud SLA will be limited as a result of this adoption. Several new features must also be introduced to accommodate the changing technology domain and time. With the widespread adoption of cloud computing, for example, trust should be a key component of the SLA. This section lists the main parameters that should be included in the cloud SLA and defines them in terms of the cloud. This work focuses on four requirements related to a CSLAT (cloud services: Availability, interoperability, reliability and trust). Additionally, a template is suggested that integrates specified parameters and aims for filling the divergence between current SLA templates and the specifications. A list of issues that should be answered in a cloud SLA is also given.

4.3.1 Availability

For organizations that have resources in the cloud, availability is a significant concern. The benefits of cloud computing contexts are lost if the availability of services on the cloud is not valued highly. Despite technological advances, many outages have occurred in recent years, demonstrating that such lapses cannot be ignored. As a result, one of the motivators for the appropriate development of cloud computing for an organization is to have ultimate potential availability, while maintaining the same service quality [21–23].

When a device is requested for use, availability refers to the likelihood that it will perform as anticipated. In other words, availability represents the likelihood that a device will not malfunction or need repair when it is required. Availability can be viewed as a behavior of reliability based on this concept. However, along with reliability, the system's maintainability (ease of maintenance) should be considered when determining availability. This means that when estimating availability, we should also remember the system's downtime. The availability of a system is determined by the amount of downtime, which is considered for study by Sericola and Bruno (1999):

- Point availability: Probability that the system becomes available at time t.

- Average availability: Fraction of time during a specified time period for which the system is available.

- Steady state availability: Limit of the availability function as t tends to infinity.

- Operational availability: Similar to availability but also includes the various downtimes such as administrative downtime, scheduled maintenance downtime and logistics downtime.

Of all the variations defined, point availability is appropriate for use in cloud computing for real-time systems or critical transactions where availability at a particular point in time is very important. Moreover, using the point availability function other availability values such as average availability and steady state availability can also be determined.

The following section discusses current approaches to predicting cloud service availability, followed by our proposed approach. The availability trace is a common method for predicting availability. In this case, the technique is to search for trends in historical data to forecast a host's availability. Visualization tools can be used to spot certain trends. Clustering algorithms like k-means are then utilized to distinguish machines with distinct patterns. Two binary vectors that calculate the fraction of unequal values in each dimension are used to determine similarity between hosts and centroids. Following that, a bit vector is used to generate a good and reliable description of the availability of a wide fraction of hosts over time while detecting current daily and weekly trends. These patterns are normally replicated with minor variations for several weeks. As a result, the patterns observed by the bit vector are likely to be replicated in the near future. The Jaccard index-based prediction approach [24] is another method for detecting trends in historical data. To forecast the availability of a particular machine within the scheme, this approach uses lazy learning algorithms to find the best match in a sequence pattern in historical data.

In environments like volunteer computing and grid computing, where users freely share resources and historical patterns can be detected to predict the availability of a particular host in the future, such methods can be used. However, since cloud computing is a for-profit business, predicting availability in the same way as grid and volunteer computing does not yield reliable results. We propose a method for predicting availability using probability distributions and available resources. The following considerations are taken into account in our approach:

- n: Number of operating units in system.

- η: Number of standby units.

- λ_i: Failure rate of ith unit.

- μ_i: Repair rate of ith unit.

- $m(u)$: Repair probability distribution function.

- t_r: Mean time in which failed units are replaced by standby unit.

If we think of the cloud as a system, its availability is primarily determined by the availability of its components, which include the CPU, infrastructure (servers), application, platform and network. For three service models, the reliance on a particular component for predicting cloud availability can differ (Table 4.2). The following equation gives the availability of a particular service model since these components are related in sequence (Equation 4.1):

$$A_s(t) = \prod_{i=1}^{n} A_i(t) \qquad (4.1)$$

TABLE 4.2   Various Components' Availability Concerns in the Context of Cloud

Availability	Server	Platform	Application	CPU	Network
IaaS	Needed	Not needed	Not needed	Needed	Needed
PaaS	Needed	Needed	Not needed	Needed	Needed
SaaS	Needed	Needed	Needed	Needed	Needed

where $A_s(t)$ is the service model availability and $A_i(t)$ is the ith component's availability of service model. The Markov model can be used to calculate the availability of individual cloud components. To begin, the component's states must be described as state space (S).

$$S = [s0, s1, \dots\dots, s\eta]$$ (4.2)

The number of states in S is determined by η, the number of standby units. The failure rate (λ_i) and the repair rate (μ_i) (Chow 1975) can be used to draw a state diagram once the states have been defined. Besides that, the failure rate and repair rate are both time-dependent and will vary depending on the probability distribution functions for failure rate and repair rate, respectively. For this, the exponential, Pareto and Weibull probability distribution functions (Charles 2010) can be used. The presumption here is that the likelihood of a device being in a given state is only contingent on the state it is in right now.

$$P(st \mid st-1, \dots\dots, s1) = P(st \mid st-1)$$ (4.3)

The state diagram of η nodes is depicted in Figure 4.1 (states). Each node represents one of the system's many possible states. For example, node $s0$ represents a good state in which everything is working properly, while node $s\eta$ represents a fail state in which Markov's process has come to an

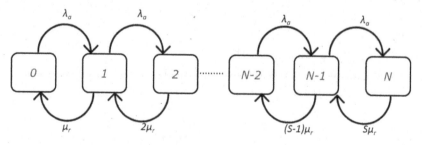

FIGURE 4.1   State transition diagram.

end. States $s1$ to $s\eta - 1$ are also considered effective, with the exception that only a few of the standby units are operational in these states. Each branch of the transformation path is labeled with a failure rate λ_i, indicating a failure that results in a state change. The failure rate mu can further be mapped out in the same way as the repair rate (μ_i). Such rates are referred to as transfer probabilities and are thus abbreviated as

$$q(x, y) = P(st + 1 = x \mid st = y) \text{ for } x, y \in S \qquad (4.4)$$

The transformation kernel is formed by combining these transaction probabilities into a matrix $\{q(s, s')\}$. Here, the element (si, sj) is the transition rate from state si to state sj, where $si = sj$. For $si = sj$ the element is a negative value of the summation of all the other values of the row (Charles 2010). A vector can be specified as to express the distribution of availability among possible states at time t.

$$\pi(t) = \left[Ps0(t), Ps1(t), ..., Ps\eta(t) \right] \qquad (4.5)$$

The probability of the component being in state $s0$ at time t is given by $Ps0(t)$. Assume the machine availability at time unit 1 is 100 percent. Since state $s0$ denotes that the system is completely operational with no failures, the likelihood of the system being in this state is 1. This is given as

$$\pi(1) = \begin{bmatrix} 1, & 0, & 0, & ...., & 0 \end{bmatrix} \qquad (4.6)$$

Therefore,

$$\pi(2) = \pi(1) * q \qquad (4.7)$$

Finally, subsequent to generalizing Equation 4.7, availability at time unit t can be specified as

$$\pi(t) = \pi(1) * q^{t-1} \qquad (4.8)$$

The dissemination of availability at different states is given by the equation above. As a result, component availability can be represented as the number of the probabilities of effective states, i.e.,

$$A_i(t) = \sum_{i=0}^{\eta-1} P(s_i(t)) \qquad (4.9)$$

4.3.2 Reliability

Generally, reliability is characterized as the likelihood that the system in review will act as anticipated for a given time period or at a specific point in time when utilized in conjunction with specified operating circumstances. One of the most critical problems addressed by almost every provider's SLA in cloud computing is reliability. Cloud service providers, on the other hand, have various viewpoints on its meaning (when it comes to availability, uptime or resilience), different options to quantify it (networks, virtual platforms and servers), different time periods to consider and extensively differing assurance terms (response time, resolution time) [15]. Customers are put at risk because of this uncertainty, so the reliability concept must be extremely accurate [9].

Next, we have proposed a method for identifying various parameters that can be used to estimate a cloud service's reliability. An SoA of a cloud computing system is shown (Figure 4.2), that is further a popular representation of the majority of current cloud service systems. A cloud management system (CMS) is made up of a set of servers that can be distributed or centralized. When a customer makes a request for a specific cloud service, the request is queued into a request queue. The CMS scheduler then spools a request from the queue and schedules the service to a server based on the availability information from the 'Resource Manager'.

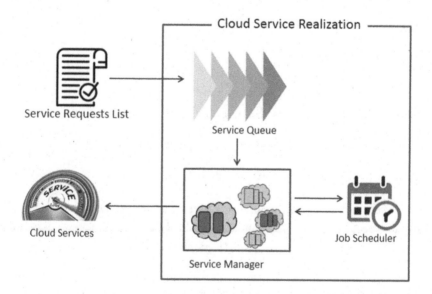

FIGURE 4.2   Cloud computing management system.

We begin by examining the various types of failure, then proceed to our method for predicting reliability.

Cloud computing device failures: Timeout, overflow, data resource missing, software failure, computing resource missing, network failure, database failure and hardware failure are all examples of failures that can impact the reliability of a cloud service. All of these failures are mentioned below in brief.

Overflow: The maximum number of requests that can be kept in the request queue should be restricted. Contrarily, fresh requests would need to wait too long in the queue, increasing the likelihood of failures related to timeout. When we observe a full queue, new work is declined, and the user is unable to receive service, resulting in a failure related to overflow.

Timeout: The application protocol or the customer normally sets the due date for the cloud service. The timeout failure occurs when the request in the queue has been waiting for more than the allotted time. Consequently, such requests of timeout will be removed from the queue, with no effect on subsequent requests.

Software failure: The subtasks are software programs that run on different resources and consist of flaws related to software.

Database failure: The database which holds necessary data resources can also malfunction, preventing the subtasks from accessing the data they need.

Hardware failure: Hardware is there for computing and data resources (e.g., servers), which may also fail.

Network failure: Communication channels can be disrupted either physically or logically when subtasks access remote data, resulting in network failure, particularly when big datasets are released over long periods of time.

All the above-mentioned failures can be classified into two groups as follows:

i) Request stage failures: Timeout and overflow failures.

ii) Execution stage failures: Database failure, network failure, hardware failure and software failures.

Failures in Group (i) can happen before or after the job request is successfully allocated to computing or data resources; failures in Group (ii) can happen after the job request has been successfully assigned and during the execution of subtasks. The modeling of cloud service reliability can be separated in two parts: Modeling the reliability at the request stage and modeling the reliability at the execution stage.

Request stage reliability: We consider the following parameters.

Request queue capacity (N): This is the maximum number of requests that the request queue can hold. Also, it is assumed that a Poisson process is followed with the arrival rate λ. We define this probability $P(x{:}\lambda)$ as λa for brevity.

Due time for a service (Td): This is the amount of time allotted from the time a work request is sent to the time the job is completed.

Mean service time (μ): The requests are served by several scheduled servers. We consider that all these servers are homogeneous with similar equipment, schemes and structures. Let us consider that total S homogeneous scheduled servers are running simultaneously to serve the requests. Each scheduled server's time to complete one request is presumed to obey a probability distribution function that can be determined by examining the service's historical data. With the above-mentioned consideration, we model the request queue as the Markov process, and a schematic of the Markov modeling of the request queue is shown in Figure 4.3.

In Figure 4.3, state n ($n = 0, 1, \ldots, N$) represents the number of requests in the queue. Note that the transition probability from state n to state to state $n + 1$ is λa for ($n = 0, 1, \ldots, N - 1$). The arrival of a new request, however, causes the request queue to overload at state N, so the request is dropped and the queue remains at state N. Now, with the probability μr that a service will be completed by a schedule server within the due time Td, there is a state change, which is proportional to the number of services currently run by the service schedulers. On the other hand, if $n \le S$,

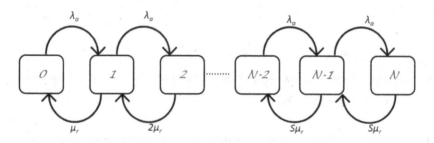

FIGURE 4.3   CMS request queue Markov model.

then n requests can be instantly serviced by the S schedule servers, so the departure rate of any one request is equal to $n\mu r$. If $n > S$, only S requests are being simultaneously served by schedule servers, so the departure rate is $S\mu r$. Let qn denote the steady-state probability of the system at any state n ($n = 0, 1, \ldots, N$). In order to calculate the values of qn, we have to solve the following equalities:

$$\text{For } n = 0 \text{ or } 1 : \text{la } q0 = \mu r \, q1 \tag{4.10}$$

$$\text{For } n = 1 \text{ to } S-1 : \lambda a \, q_{i-1} + (i+1)\mu r \, q_{i+1} = \lambda a \, qi + i \cdot \mu r \, qi \tag{4.11}$$

$$\text{For } n = S \text{ to } N-1 : \lambda a \, q_{i-1} + S\mu r \, q_{i+1} = \lambda a \, qi + S\mu r \, qi \tag{4.12}$$

$$\text{For } i = N : \lambda a \, q_{N-1} = S\mu r \, qN \tag{4.13}$$

Since, the system will be at any one state, at any instant, we have

$$\sum_{i=0}^{N-1} qi = 1 \tag{4.14}$$

We can solve these equations to determine the values of qi ($i = 0, 1, \ldots, N$). The probability that overflow failure will not occur is

$$\sum_{i=0}^{N-1} qi \tag{4.15}$$

Now, considering the service time of a schedule server follows the probability distribution function, say $P(t)$, the probability that a job in a state will be serviced within a due time is

$$P_r(t \leq T_d) = \int_0^{T_d} P(t)dt \tag{4.16}$$

Therefore, the probability of non-occurrence of timeout or overflow is

$$R_{Stage1} = \sum_{i=0}^{N-1} q_i * \int_0^{T_d} P(t)dt \tag{4.17}$$

This R_{Stage1} denotes the reliability at the request stage.

Execution stage reliability: The execution stage fails when one or more of the components, such as hardware, software, database, software or a communication connection, fails. As a result, each component has its own failure rate. It's worth noting that no changes to the software source code are made during the operating process, so the software failure rate remains constant [14]. In the operational phase of hardware with electronic components, a constant failure rate is usually observed. If λi is the failure rate of any ith element, then τi is the element's reliability if it runs for τi time (Charles 2010).

$$R_i = e^{-\lambda_i \cdot T_i} \tag{4.18}$$

To measure the execution time of the various types of elements used in the cloud service, we take into account the characteristics mentioned in Table 4.3. We may measure the execution time in each based on the above requirements, as shown in Table 4.4. We can measure the execution stage reliability using the failure probabilities for each variable in a service, as shown in the equation below.

$$R_{Stage2} = \frac{Y}{\forall i} e^{-\lambda_i \cdot \tau_i} \tag{4.19}$$

Therefore, for a cloud infrastructure to become successfully deployed, both stages (request and execution) should have considerable security. Once the reliability of execution and request stages is determined, we will combine the reliability of the two stages to obtain the service's reliability as

$$R_{Service} = R_{Stage1} \, R_{Stage2} \tag{4.20}$$

TABLE 4.3   Characterization of Different Elements Involved in a Cloud Service

Element	Parameter
Hardware	Processing speed: π_i (in MIPS)
Software	Workload: ω_j (no. of instructions)
Data resource	Amount of data download/upload: α_k (in megabytes)
Communication	Bandwidth: β_m (in bits per second)

TABLE 4.4   Calculation of Time Component in Different Elements

Element	Execution time
Software	$\tau_i(\text{software}) = \dfrac{\text{Software workload}}{\text{Processing speed}} = \dfrac{\omega_i}{\pi_j}$ (when ith software is running on jth hardware)
Communication	$\tau_i(\text{communication}) = \dfrac{\text{Amount of data}}{\text{bandwidth}} = \dfrac{\alpha_j}{\beta_i}$ (when mth communication link is transmitting on ith datarce)
Hardware	$\sum \tau_i(\text{hardware}) = \displaystyle\sum_{j \to k}^{\tau_j}(\text{software}) + \sum \tau_k(\text{communication})$ (running jth software and kth communication link)
Data resource	$\tau_i = \displaystyle\sum_{j}^{\tau_j}(\text{communication})$ (working time of data resource includes total communication time the resource is utilized)

4.4 CONCLUSION

In cloud computing-based service provisioning, quality of service is a major concern. The SLA has been identified as a critical artifact for ensuring cloud service QoS. This chapter attempts to fill the void. The proposed details on parameters such as availability and reliability are viewed as keys to ensuring QoS. The methodology for calculating these metrics in the context of a cloud service between customers and providers is also explained in depth. Furthermore, the detailed analysis of quality attributes provides the ability to transcend the flaws of a heterogeneous world. The attributes description can be used in a cloud monitoring tool.

REFERENCES

1. Wu, L., & Buyya, R. (2012). Service level agreement (SLA) in utility computing systems. In *Performance and Dependability in Service Computing: Concepts, Techniques and Research Directions* (pp. 1–25). IGI Global.
2. Keller, A., & Ludwig, H. (2003). The WSLA framework: Specifying and monitoring service level agreements for web services. *Journal of Network and Systems Management*, 11(1), 57–81.
3. Lamanna, D. D., Skene, J., & Emmerich, W. (2003, January). Slang: A language for defining service level agreements. In Ninth IEEE Workshop on Future Trends of Distributed Computing Systems, Proceedings (pp. 100–106). IEEE Computer Soc.

4. Tosic, V., Patel, K., & Pagurek, B. (2002, May). Wsol—web service offerings language. In International Workshop on Web Services, E-Business, and the Semantic Web (pp. 57–67). Springer, Berlin, Heidelberg.

5. Charles, E. (2010), *An Introduction to Reliability and Maintainability Engineering*, McGraw Hill, New York.

6. Chow, D. K. (1975). Availability of some repairable computer systems. *IEEE Transactions on Reliability*, 24(1), 64–66.

7. Patel, P., Ranabahu, A. H., & Sheth, A. P. (2009). Service level agreement in cloud computing. URL: https://corescholar.libraries.wright.edu/knoesis /78.

8. Comuzzi, M., Kotsokalis, C., Spanoudakis, G., & Yahyapour, R. (2009, July). Establishing and monitoring SLAs in complex service based systems. In 2009 IEEE International Conference on Web Services (pp. 783–790). IEEE.

9. Dahbur, K., Mohammad, B., & Tarakji, A. B. (2011, April). A survey of risks, threats and vulnerabilities in cloud computing. In Proceedings of the 2011 International Conference on Intelligent Semantic Web-services and Applications (pp. 1–6).

10. Rawat, P. S., Dimri, P., Gupta, P., & Saroha, G. P. (2021). Resource provisioning in scalable cloud using bio-inspired artificial neural network model. *Applied Soft Computing*, 99, 106876.

11. Eng, K., Muhammed, A., Mohamed, M. A., & Hasan, S. (2020). A hybrid heuristic of variable neighbourhood descent and great deluge algorithm for efficient task scheduling in grid computing. *European Journal of Operational Research*, 284(1), 75–86.

12. Ferrer, A. J., Hernández, F., Tordsson, J., Elmroth, E., Ali-Eldin, A., Zsigri, C., ... & Sheridan, C. (2012). OPTIMIS: A holistic approach to cloud service provisioning. *Future Generation Computer Systems*, 28(1), 66–77.

13. Rawat, P. S., Gupta, P., Dimri, P., & Saroha, G. P. (2020). Power efficient resource provisioning for cloud infrastructure using bio-inspired artificial neural network model. *Sustainable Computing: Informatics and Systems*, 28, 100431.

14. Goel, A. L., & Okumoto, K. (1979). Time-dependent error-detection rate model for software reliability and other performance measures. *IEEE Transactions on Reliability*, 28(3), 206–211.

15. Hogan, M., Liu, F., Sokol, A., & Tong, J. (2011). NIST cloud computing standards roadmap. *NIST Special Publication*, 35, 6–11.

16. Armbrust, M., Fox, A., Griffith, R., Joseph, A. D., Katz, R., Konwinski, A., ... & Zaharia, M. (2010). A view of cloud computing. *Communications of the ACM*, 53(4), 50–58.

17. Nurmi, D., Wolski, R., Grzegorczyk, C., Obertelli, G., Soman, S., Youseff, L., & Zagorodnov, D. (2008). Eucalyptus: A technical report on an elastic utility computing architecture linking your programs to useful systems. In *UCSB Technical Report*.

18. Jin, L. J., Machiraju, V., & Sahai, A. (2002). Analysis on service level agreement of web services. *HP*, June, 19, 1–13.

19. Andrieux, A., Czajkowski, K., Dan, A., Keahey, K., Ludwig, H., Nakata, T., ... & Xu, M. (2007, March). Web services agreement specification (WS-Agreement). In Open Grid Forum (Vol. 128, No. 1, p. 216).
20. Brandic, I., Music, D., Leitner, P., & Dustdar, S. (2009, August). Vieslaf framework: Enabling adaptive and versatile sla-management. In International Workshop on Grid Economics and Business Models (pp. 60–73). Springer, Berlin, Heidelberg.
21. Schnorr, L. M., Legrand, A., & Vincent, J. M. (2010). *Visualization and Detection of Resource Usage Anomalies in Large Scale Distributed Systems* (Doctoral dissertation, INRIA).
22. Sericola, B. (1999). Availability analysis of repairable computer systems and stationarity detection. *IEEE Transactions on Computers*, 48(11), 1166–1172.
23. Theilmann, W., Happe, J., Kotsokalis, C., Edmonds, A., Kearney, K., & Lambea, J. (2010). A reference architecture for multi-level sla management. *Journal of Internet Engineering*, 4(1), 289–298.
24. Rahman, M., Hassan, M. R., & Buyya, R. (2010). Jaccard index based availability prediction in enterprise grids. *Procedia Computer Science*, 1(1), 2707–2716.

CHAPTER 5

Neural Network and Deep Learning-Based Resource Allocation Model for Multilayered Cloud

Sanjit Bhagat and Punit Gupta

CONTENTS

DOI: 10.1201/9781003185376-5

5.1 INTRODUCTION

The deep learning algorithms have the ability to learn through past datasets and predict the future best possible solutions. So, involving the deep learning algorithms will make cloud more feasible in every aspect, whether it is cost, energy or resource allocation. The decisions taken after training from the past dataset will improve the accuracy and minimize the time as there is no human interaction. The algorithm learns by itself. All the cloud models are possible to implement via neural network and deep learning concepts; there is no need for additional regular algorithms. Artificial neural networks/feed forward neural networks (ANN), convolutional neural networks (CNN) and recurrent neural networks (RNN) are techniques used to develop these intelligent algorithms.

Cloud is growing rapidly, so the data interpretation and complexations are too. It is quite difficult to handle such a vast amount of data via normal programs and functionality; it will take a long time and manpower to handle the data. Self-learning algorithms are a good solution for this as they can process, interpret, summarize and produce the outcomes in a very short time with a good reliability level. Cloud computing is just a scalable system that can deal with any amount of data any time. Technologies and techniques always need to be improved as a large amount of data is being transported and processed onto cloud. These intelligent algorithms will make cloud more reliable, scalable and distributed while making it energy, cost and power efficient.

In this chapter we will focus on the resource allocation issues and factors affecting resource allocation. We will discuss cloud, deep learning algorithms and some review works on cloud and DL and proposed hybrid models.

5.1.1 Cloud Delivery/Deployment Model

Cloud computing is divided into four deployment/delivery models as per NIST (Figure 5.1).

- **Public cloud**: This is operated by a third party, which delivers resources like servers and storage over the Internet. Microsoft Azure is an example of a public cloud. In a public cloud all the hardware, software and infrastructure are managed by the provider. A user can only access these services and manage his/her account using a web browser.

- **Private cloud**: As the name indicates, this is a dedicated cloud service where resources are exclusively used by a single business or organization. A private cloud can be located on the company site, or a third party may be paid to manage it for the organization specifically.

- **Hybrid cloud**: This combines public and private clouds, so that data and applications can be moved from public to private or vice versa. It provides great flexibility and more deployment options to the existing infrastructure.

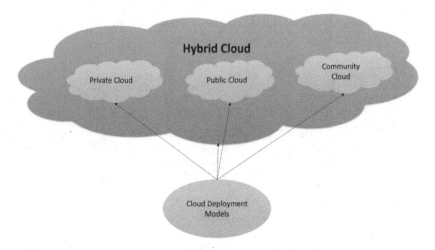

FIGURE 5.1   Cloud computing deployment model.

- **Community cloud**: Unlike the types of cloud defined above, a community cloud is there for the exclusive use of a particular community that has shared concerns or a common purpose.

5.1.2 Cloud Service/Model Type

The three service types defined by NIST are SaaS, PaaS and IaaS, focus on a specific layer: The hardware, the system software (platform) and the application respectively. The three service models are described as follows (Figure 5.2):

- **Software as a service (Saas)**: This service provides software applications over the Internet on demand. The user need not to install this on their local machine. The software can be accessed by the user through a web browser. The application cannot be controlled by the user, it can only be used. All the maintenance and updates are handled by the provider.

- **Platform as a service (PaaS)**: This refers to the cloud service which provides the environment for developing, testing and delivering the software applications. The user is able to install and manipulate the applications on the provided platform. PaaS includes services like server, storage, networking and development tools.

- **Infrastructure as a service (IaaS)**: IaaS provides whole infrastructure as a service, it can quickly scale up and down on demand, and you pay for what you use. The user can purchase, install, configure and manage their own software, operating system and any application, while the infrastructure is managed by the service provider.

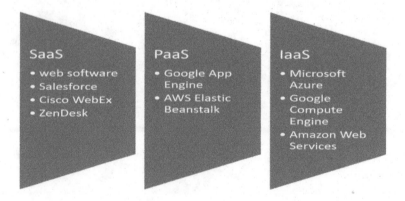

FIGURE 5.2 Cloud service providers at different service levels.

5.1.3 Current Issues in Cloud

Although cloud is quite capable of handling the migration of the data from the organizations, the increasing amount of data and processing leads to poor resource utilization and hence increases in cost, power and energy consumption. Some of the general cloud issues are given below.

5.1.3.1 Cost Management

The distributive property of cloud helps to save costs for an organization. Cloud can help organizations to save money as they don't need to invest extra for the hardware or resource. The issue is the on-demand and scalable nature of cloud that can lead to poor prediction of required resources and costs.

5.1.3.2 Security Issues

Increasing amounts of data and the migration of organizations generate major security concerns. Security is becoming one of the most major issues in cloud, as organizations are not able to see the exact location of the stored data. This may lead to data breach issues. Although security is improving rapidly, still there are trust issues to do with migrating sensitive and proprietary data on cloud.

5.1.3.3 Migration

The process of moving data from local to cloud or vice versa is migration. Moving a new application is a step-by-step process that is quite simple, but moving an existing application in a cloud environment is still a challenging task.

5.1.3.4 Performance

The organizations that have moved to the cloud are totally dependent on the service provider as there is no physical existence of the hardware resources and there is a lack of control over the resources. So, maintaining a smooth performance is also a challenge for the cloud system whether it is a migration process or a resource allocation process.

5.1.3.5 Multi-Cloud (Hybrid Cloud) Management

Public cloud is still not trustable for the security and privacy of private and confidential data. So, a mix of private and public cloud is the first choice for organizations where they can store the confidential data on the private cloud and the rest on the public cloud to save costs and energy. Managing this type of cloud is also a challenge for the service providers.

5.1.3.6 Resource Allocation and Management

Moving the organization increases the work load on the cloud environment. Although cloud technologies are improving rapidly, still it is not feasible for everyone as it is difficult to maintain the performance with this flexible demand and service approach. It may increase the cost and time of resources, and there will be no proper utilization of resources. A better way to optimize the resources is still needed.

5.1.4 Factors Affecting Resource Allocation

5.1.4.1 Resource Scaling

Scaling is the ability to adjust the resources up and down according to the demand of the user. The resources are reduced when not required and added if required; this affects the cost and energy efficiency of the cloud system. The proper management of resources will lead to a better cloud performance. Gartner defines auto-scaling as follows:

> Auto-scaling automates the expansion or contraction of system capacity that is available for applications and is a commonly desired feature in cloud IaaS and PaaS offerings. When feasible, technology buyers should use it to match provisioned capacity to application demand and save costs [2].

From an academic point of view auto-scaling is the capability of cloud to dynamically provide the virtualized resources. The resources used by cloud can automatically increase or decrease.

5.1.4.2 Energy Utilization

Better energy utilization is another major factor that affects the resource optimization and thus the cloud performance. Increasing demand and better performance will decrease the energy efficiency, hence the increase in cost.

Due to the increase in data centers and their various computing operations, it is necessary to have an energy-efficient resource allocation mechanism. These centers lead to the release of large quantities of carbon emissions. Ashkan Paya and Dan C. Marinescu stated a related solution in their paper 'Energy-Aware Load Balancing and Application Scaling for the Cloud Ecosystem' [3]. The proper management of resources will lead to an energy-efficient cloud system. The decrease in energy consumption will reduce the operational expenses and make cloud more profitable.

5.1.4.3 Virtual Machine (VM) Migration

The cloud is a distributed environment where the user can migrate his/her work on different machines that completes the execution quickly. Virtualization means multiple logical machines on a single physical machine. In migration a VM moves from one physical machine to another. Migration can be either offline or online (live). In offline migration the machine is stopped until the migration process is complete while in online (live) migration there is no interruption in client service while the migration is in process. Live migration has been significantly used in energy reduction, load balancing and dynamic allocation of resources.

To migrate VM, the entire VM state has to be transferred from the source to the target. VM includes permanent storage, volatile storage, the state of connected devices and the internal state of the virtual CPUs. Permanent storage not need be moved because it is provided by network-attached storage (NAS). The state of the CPU and the virtual devices having a small size can easily be transferred to the target host. The main issue in live migration is to transfer main memory (i.e., volatile storage) because it contains data in gigabytes [4].

The importance of the cloud is increasing exponentially. Gartner forecasts that the cloud services market will grow 17.3% in 2019 ($206.2 billion) and by 2022, 90% of organizations will be using cloud services [2] (Table 5.1).

TABLE 5.1　Worldwide Public Cloud Service Revenue Forecast (Billions of US Dollars) [2]

	2018	2019	2020	2021	2022
Cloud business process services (BPaaS)	41.7	43.7	46.9	50.2	53.8
Cloud application infrastructure services (PaaS)	26.4	32.2	39.7	48.3	58.0
Cloud application services (SaaS)	85.7	99.5	116.0	133.0	151.1
Cloud management and security services	10.5	12.0	13.8	15.7	17.6
Cloud system infrastructure services (IaaS)	32.4	40.3	50.0	61.3	74.1
Total market	**196.7**	**227.8**	**266.4**	**308.5**	**354.6**

5.2 INTRODUCTION TO NEURAL NETWORKS

The artificial neural network is inspired by the functionality of the human brain. ANN is a set of algorithms which functions like the human brain to recognize patterns. Neural networks are fed with some raw input data that is interpreted by clustering, precepting or labeling it. ANN can recognize all real-world objects and patterns such as images, sound, texts, etc. ANN helps in classification, clustering and grouping unlabeled data.

To expand the name, neural refers to brain cell neurons in the human body and network refers to interconnected components. Neurons in the human body transmit signals to the brain, but the important thing is human brain learns from the experience and train the data according to the past experience. In the same way we want to make an artificial machine work on the concept of the human brain, called a neural network. In an artificial neural network there will be artificial neurons which transmit the signal and train the data to generate a better output. The neural network can be used in areas like recognizing things like a human brain does, for example data classification and pattern recognition.

Kinds of neural network:

- **Artificial neural networks (ANN).**

- **Convolution neural networks (CNN).**

- **Recurrent neural networks (RNN).**

5.2.1 Artificial Neural Networks (ANN)

This is the simplest kind of neural network. An artificial neural network is a collection of various neural networks at each level. Inputs in an artificial neural network are processed in the forward direction. So, an artificial neural network is also called a feedforward neural network. These networks are universal function approximators as they can learn any kind of nonlinear function. The mapping is done using the weights given to the input to generate the output. The activation function helps the network to understand the relation between input and output.

ANN has the following three layers (Figure 5.3):

- **Input layer:** In the input layer of an artificial neural network, the inputs are accepted. The inputs which are accepted and forwarded

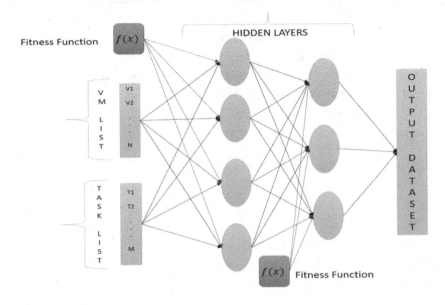

FIGURE 5.3   ANN architecture for proposed model.

to the next layer. In our case the input will consist of the following variables.

- **Hidden layer**: The hidden layer of the artificial neural network has no connection to the outer world; that is why it is called hidden layer. It processes the input which is forwarded by the input layer.

- **Output layer**: The output layer of the artificial neural network generates the output processed by the hidden layer.

In our case

$$\$\text{vmlist} = \left[1, 2, 3, 4 \dots\dots\dots\dots\dots n \right]$$

$$\$\text{tasklist} = \left[1, 2, 3, 4 \dots\dots\dots\dots\dots m \right]$$

are random input parameters that we will pass into our ANN algorithm; the hidden layer will process the input data and pass it to the next layer if available. At the final stage we will get the output dataset. These learning-based algorithms will learn from the previous datasets (Training Dataset) and predict the optimal solutions of the problem. The fitness function acts as the threshhold point for the hidden and input layers to process data.

5.2.2 Convolution Neural Network (CNN)

The convolutional neural network is mainly used for image classification. Convolutional neural network can produce the data from the images and can differentiate an image from another. The building blocks of convolutional neural networks are the kernels. Kernels are also known as filters. Using the convolutional operations kernels or filters are used to extract the relevant features from the input.

5.2.3 Recurrent Neural Networks (RNN)

Recurrent neural networks are extended version of the artificial neural networks. Unlike artificial neural networks which process forward at each layer, in the recurrent neural network the iterative constraint at the hidden layer is added. So, by the iterative constraint we can access the information from the previous iteration and train the data according to the past iteration. As it has the recurrent connection on the hidden layer, it is known as a recurrent neural network. The previous output is considered as input for the next layer.

- **Input layer**: The input layer takes the input in recurrent neural networks.

- **Recurrent layer**: In the recurrent layer the inputs are processed and then iterated to generate a better output.

- **Output layer**: This layer generates the output processed by recurrent layers.

The use of deep learning with cloud will surely produce better outcomes in comparison to the traditional approaches. The above algorithms are classified according to their objectives and the way of working. The basic functionality is to give input with some weight and a thrash hold point, and pass it to the hidden layer which will process the input with activation function and then produce output. Each layer will have their own bias point.

5.3 INTRODUCTION TO THE GENETIC ALGORITHM

This algorithm is a search-based heuristic algorithm, that selects the object on a fitness criterion for further processing. The GA consists of five phases:

1. **Initial population:** This is the set of the possible solutions of the given problem. Every element of the set is characterized with some parameters. While deciding the initial population, the diversity and

population size should be kept in mind. The population size is a random vector. The initialization can be done in two ways:

1. **Random initialization**: Where the solution is given randomly without prior knowledge.

2. **Heuristic initialization**: The solutions are given on some prior known factors; this may cause similarity and less diversity in the solution.

We are using random initialization in our case,

$$VM\left[\text{list}\right] = \left\{Vm1, Vm2, Vm3\& \& ., Vm_n\right\}$$

$$P\left[n\right] = \left\{P1, P2, P3, \ldots\ldots\ldots, P_n\right\}$$

Figure 5.4 is a single solution; we will generate a set of n solutions from the population

$$S_n = \left\{\left[\,Vm\left[\text{List}\right]_1, P\left[n\right]_1\right], \left[\,Vm\left[\text{List}\right]_2, P\left[n\right]_2\right],\right.$$

$$\left.\ldots\ldots\ldots,\left[Vm\left[\text{List}\right]_i, P\left[n\right]_j\right]\right\};$$

$$S_n = \left\{S1, S2, S3,\ldots\ldots\ldots Sn\right\}$$

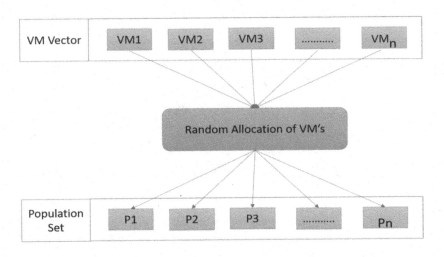

FIGURE 5.4   Random allocations of VMs to the population vector.

Where
Vm is an array of virtual machines.
P is the population set.
And S_n is the set of solutions.

After the initial population is determined, a predefined fitness function is applied to the initial population.

2. **Fitness function**: This is a predefined function that determines the fitness of individual elements of the initial population set. The selection of the individual is based on the fitness score. The fitness function should be fast enough to calculate the fitness of the given solution as we may have to repeat it multiple times until an optimal solution is found. Fitness may be exact or approximate depending on the case.

   After the fitness function is applied, we will get the list of fit solutions determined by the fitness function (Figure 5.5).

   That is,

$$F_n = \{S1,\ S3,\ldots\ldots\ldots\ldots Sn\};$$

F_n is the set of fit solutions.

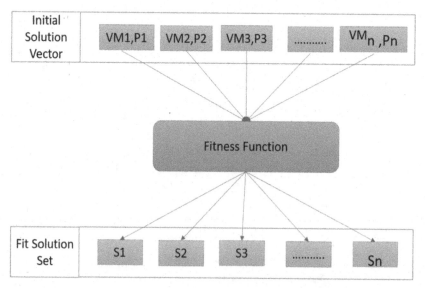

FIGURE 5.5   Generating fit solution set after fitness function is applied.

3. **Parent selection**: Selection is a crucial part of a genetic algorithm as, if we select the fittest possible solution, it may take upon the entire population hence resulting in **premature convergence**. Good diversity maintenance is necessary for successful GA. There are various ways to select the solution.

   a. **Fitness proportionate selection**:

   In this every solution can become a parent with the probability proportional to its fitness. Hence the fitter solutions will have higher chances of selection. There are two possible models for this type of selection:

   1. **Roulette wheel selection**: A fixed point is defined on the circumference of the wheel. After the rotation, whichever region stops in front of the point is elected as parent. The greater fitness solution will cover a large region and hence have a high chance of selection.

   2. **Stochastic universal sampling**: We will have multiple fixed points; therefore all the parents will be chosen in one spin.

   b. **Tournament selection**:

   In n-way tournament selection, n individual solutions are selected from the population. The process is repeated until the fittest parent is selected. This method can work with negative values too.

   c. **Rank selection**:

   When the fitness of the individuals is very close to each other. In this the fitness value is almost not considerable as all the sets have the same fitness value. The higher ranked is preferred.

4. **Crossover**: In this more than one parent is selected and one or more set is generated having the parent attributes. The crossover is applied with a high probability. There are various ways to perform a crossover.

5. **One-point crossover**: Here the random point is selected from the parent(s), and a new solution is generated with the swapping process.

a. **Multi-point crossover**: It is advanced to the one-point crossover; in this we will have multiple random points to generate a new solution.

b. **Uniform crossover**: In this there is no random point. We decide whether the property of parent will be selected or not by flipping a coin.

c. **Whole arithmetic recombination**: This takes a weighted average of two parents by the formulae

$$Child1 = \alpha \cdot x + (1-\alpha) \cdot Y$$
$$Child1 = \alpha \cdot x + (1-\alpha) \cdot Y$$

d. **Davis's order crossover (OX1)**: This is a permutation-based crossover that transmits relative information to the new solutions. It works as follows:

1. Define two random points in the parent and copy the segment between points and move it to the first new solution.

2. Now from the second point in the second parent copy the unused content and move to the first solution.

3. Repeat for the second solution in reverse parent manner.

6. **Mutation**: This process makes a random small change in the parent solution to generate a new solution. This occurs to maintain the diversity in the initial population set and works on low probability. The most commonly used mutations are

a. **Bit flip mutation**: We select some random bits and flip them to get a new solution. Mostly used in binary encoded GA.

b. **Random setting**: In this a random integer value is assigned to a randomly selected solution.

c. **Swap mutation**: This combination-based encoding selects two random points from the parent and swaps them to generate a new solution.

d. **Scramble mutation**: In this a subset of the solution is selected and scrambled/shuffled to generate a new solution.

e. **Inversion mutation**: Similar to the scramble selection mutation, we choose a subset but instead of shuffling we invert the list to generate a new solution.

7. **Termination condition**: When the genetic algorithm provides a set of solutions, the algorithm is terminated. In the start the GA tends to be very fast, but at later stages it comes to a saturation point where the improvements are very small. Termination is usually done when we are very close to optimal solution. Usually, the following points should be considered at termination

   1. When there are no improvements for n iterations.

   2. If we reach an absolute number of generations.

   3. When the solution has reached the predefined criteria.

5.4 PROPOSED MODEL 1 (A HYBRID GA AND NAÏVE BAYES MODEL FOR OPTIMIZATION)

Our aim is to merge these two algorithms into one to generate a hybrid algorithm that will save the total execution time of a task as well as improve the prediction that will help into proper resource optimization while saving the execution time (Figure 5.6).

At first, we will generate a random list from all the available VMs and a training dataset. This will be our input to any genetic algorithm; the dataset will be used to train the algorithm for the further selection. And later on, a naïve Bayes algorithm will use a probability method for the final selections of the output dataset. A fitness function will be used to find out the fitness of every object.

5.5 WHALE OPTIMIZATION ALGORITHM (WOA)

WOA was proposed by Jalili and Lewis for optimizing numerical problems (Mir Jalili & Lewi, 2016). It is a meta-heuristic algorithm that functions like humpback whales. The foraging behavior is known as bubble-net feeding. The prey are small fishes close to the surface. The foraging is done by creating distinctive bubbles along a circle. The whole process is done in three stages: Coral loop (encircling prey), lobtail (bubble-net attacking method (exploitation phase)) and capture loop (search for prey (exploration phase)).

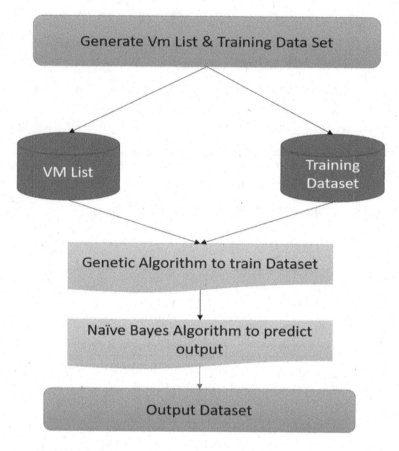

FIGURE 5.6   Proposed model for the hybrid algorithm.

5.5.1 Mathematical Model

5.5.1.1 Stage 1: Encircling Prey

The first stage is to recognize the location of prey and mark them. The current best search agent is considered to be the target prey. After deciding the current best solution, the other solutions will try to update their position towards the current best solution. This process is formulated as

$$\vec{D} = \left| \vec{C} \cdot \vec{X}^{*}(t) - \vec{X}(t) \right|$$

$$\vec{X}(t+1) = \left| \vec{X}^{*}(t) - \vec{A} \cdot \vec{D} \right|$$

where

t indicates the current iteration.

X^{*} is the position vector of the best solution obtained so far at iteration t.

$\vec{X}$ is the position vector of each agent.

The coefficient vectors $\vec{A}$ and $\vec{C}$ are calculated as:

$$\vec{A} = 2\vec{a} \cdot r - \vec{a}$$

$$\vec{C} = 2r$$

where
$\vec{a}$ is linearly decreased from 2 to 0 over the course of the iteration.
r is a random vector number $[0,1]$.

5.5.1.2 Stage 2: Bubble-Net Attacking (Exploitation Phase)
The exploitation phase is a combination of two approaches.

a) **Shrinking Encircling Mechanism**:

This mechanism is achieved by decreasing the value of $\vec{a}$; the fluctuation range of $\vec{A}$ is also decreased by $\vec{a}$.

We can say, $\vec{A}$ is a random value in the interval $[-a,a]$ where a is decreased from 2 to 0 over the process of iterations.

b) **Spiral Updating Position**:

In this step an equation is created between the position of whale and the target to create a helix-shaped movement; the equation is as follows

$$\vec{D'} = \left| \vec{X}^*(t) - \vec{X}(t) \right|$$

$$\vec{X}(t+1) = \vec{D'} \cdot e^{bl} \cdot \cos(2\pi l) + \vec{X}^*(t)$$

where
$\vec{D'}$ is the distance between the whale and target.
b is a constant that defines the logarithmic shape.
l is random in $[-1,1]$.

A humpback whale moves along a spiral-shaped path while shrinking the circle at the same time. If we assume there are 50-50 chances to choose between shrinking encircling or spiral model movement during an iteration, then:

$$\vec{X}(t+1) = \begin{cases} \vec{X}^*(t) - \vec{A}.\vec{D} & \text{if} \quad p < 0.5; \\ \vec{D}' \cdot e^{bl} \cdot \cos(2\pi l) + \vec{X}^*(t) & \text{if} \quad p \geq 0.5, \end{cases}$$

where p is a random number in [0,1].

5.5.1.3 Stage 3: Capture Loop (Search for Prey (Exploration Phase))

In the bubble-net method the target is not defined; hence the prey is searched randomly. The variation of $\vec{A}$ can be used, where $-1 > \vec{A} > 1$, that forces the search agent to move far away from the reference location (whale). The position of the search agent will update according to the random chosen solution, instead of the best solution so far.

This can be formulated as:

$$\vec{D} = \left| \vec{C} \cdot \vec{X}_{rand} - \vec{X} \right|$$

$$\vec{X}(t+1) = \left| \vec{X}_{rand} - \vec{A}.\vec{D} \right|$$

Where X_{rand} is a random position vector.

WOA algorithm (pseudo code):

In the beginning there is a set of random solutions. In each iteration the search agent updates its position according to either the best solution or a randomly chosen agent. To explore and exploit the parameter is decreased from 2 to 0.

If $\vec{A} > 1$, chose a random agent, and if $\vec{A} < 1$, choose the best solution so far to update the position of search agents.

Pseudo code:

```
Input data, max_iteration , population
Initialize whales population Xi (i = 1,2,3........n)
Initialize A, C, l, a and p
```

```
Calculate the fitness of each search agent
X* = best agent at the beginning
While (It < max_iteration)
    for each search_agent
        if (p < 0.5)
            if (|A| < 1)
                update search agent with
```
$$\vec{X}(t+1)=\vec{X}^*(t)-\vec{A}\cdot\vec{D}$$
```
            else if (|A| >= 1)
                select random search agent (X_rand)
                update the current search agent with
```
$$\vec{X}(t+1)=\vec{X}_{rand}-\vec{A}\cdot\vec{D}$$
```
            end
        else if (p >= 0.5)
            update the position of current search agent with
```
$$\vec{X}(t+1)=\vec{D}'\cdot e^{bl}\cdot\cos(2\pi l)+\vec{X}^*(t)$$
```
Calculate fitness of each search agent
Update X* if better agent found
It = It+1
Update A, C, l, a and p
end while
return X*
```

We are going to propose an improvised whale optimization with ANN to achieve higher accuracy and minimum response time (Figure 5.7).

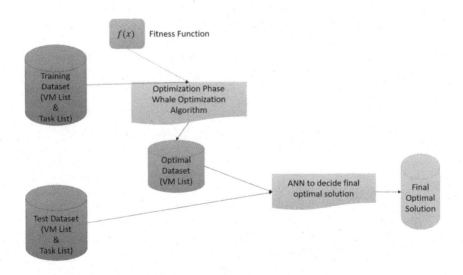

FIGURE 5.7   Proposed model architecture WOA and ANN.

WOA takes the VM list and fitness function as input with other parameters. Then it generates an optimal solution for each iteration. This list is passed to the ANN algorithm for learning purposes, and a test dataset will be passed into ANN for further prediction. Hence it will increase the accuracy and efficiency as well.

TABLE 5.2   Related Work Analysis with Cloud- and ANN-Based Approaches

	Authors	Approach	Result/Conclusion
[1]	Reshmi, R. and Saravanan	Gaussian-based adaptive least mean square filter (DoG–ALMS)	This approach improved the overall resource optimization of the network
[2]	Akki, P. and Vijayarajan, V.	Optimized neural network/ convolutional neural network with improvised BAT algorithm	Proposed approach is more power efficient in comparison with traditional BAT
[3]	Jeddi, S. and Sharifian, S.	Proposed a model to predict highly fluctuating workloads based on wavelet transform and GMDH method	Better CPU scaling and resizing
[4]	Chudasama, V. and Bhavsar	A bi-directional LSTM-based approach, predictor algorithm	This model was closer to the actual demand for resources than the other models. It is capable of optimizing the SLA violation
[5]	AbdElminaam, D.S. and Toony	A double chain quantum technology integrated into a genetic algorithm	This optimization model improved the resource optimization accuracy
[6]	Chen, S. and Fang, S	ANN-based approach for real-time scheduling	It optimized the response time for the real time scheduling
[7]	Hasan, M. and Almamun, M.	Novel self-adaptive resource allocation architecture	The model is QoS satisfactory as well as energy efficient
[8]	Kholidy, H.A.	Swarm intelligence-based prediction approach (SIBPA)	Achieved higher accuracy with good response and throughput time for better scaling decision
[9]	Lang, K. and Zhao	Cloud computing resource method based on an improved ANN model	Predicated reasonable resource scheduling accuracy
[10]	Saravanan, S. and Anbalagan	Integrated deep reinforcement learning and lion optimization algorithm	Proper resource allocation and optimization with less response time

Proposed Model 2 (WOA with ANN)

$$\$Vm \text{ list} = \left[Vm_1, Vm_2, Vm_3, \ldots\ldots\ldots\ldots Vm_n \right]$$

$$\$\text{TaskList} = \left[T_1, T_2, T_3, \ldots\ldots\ldots\ldots\ldots T_n \right]$$

$$\$\text{random}Vm = \left[1, 2, 3\ldots\ldots\ldots n \right]$$

Fitness function:

$$f(x) = \sum_{i=1}^{n} \frac{t[i]}{VM\left[randomVm[i] \right]}$$

where $t[i]$ = task length, $VM[randomVm[i]]$ = Vm at the random position.

With the help of the above parameters, WOA will generate an optimal dataset solution, that will be passed to the ANN as a training module and a test set to produce a final optimal solution based on training.

5.6 RELATED WORK

In Table 5.2 we discuss some related work with cloud- and learning-based algorithms.

5.7 CONCLUSION

The work shows the current state-of-the-art work from the field of resource allocation algorithms using nature-inspired algorithms and machine learning algorithms. The comparison shows that machine learning-based algorithms using ANN, RNN or random forest perform better than existing nature-inspired and meta-heuristic algorithms. The work shows various issues and performance parameters. The work will provide researchers with a review of current state-of-the-art work from the field of resource allocation in cloud.

REFERENCES

1. Peter Mell, and Timothy Grance, "The NIST definition of cloud computing." Sep, 2011. http://csrc.nist.gov/publications/nistpubs/800-145/SP800-145.pdf
2. Gartner Research, http://www.gartner.com/it-glossary/cloud-computing/
3. Reshmi, R., and D. Shanthi Saravanan. "Load prediction using (DoG–ALMS) for resource allocation based on IFP soft computing approach in cloud computing." *Soft Computing* 24, no. 20 (2020): 15307–15315.

4. Akki, Praveena, and V. Vijayarajan. "Energy efficient resource scheduling using optimization based neural network in mobile cloud computing." *Wireless Personal Communications* 114 (2020): 1785–1804.

5. Jeddi, Sima, and Saeed Sharifian. "A hybrid wavelet decomposer and GMDH-ELM ensemble model for network function virtualization workload forecasting in cloud computing." *Applied Soft Computing* 88 (2020): 105940.

6. Chudasama, Vipul, and Madhuri Bhavsar. "A dynamic prediction for elastic resource allocation in hybrid cloud environment." *Scalable Computing: Practice and Experience* 21, no. 4 (2020): 661–672.

7. AbdElminaam, Diaa Salama, Ahmed A. Toony, and Mohamed Taha. "Resource allocation in the cloud environment based on quantum genetic algorithm using Kalman filter with ANFIS." *IJCSNS* 20, no. 10 (2020): 10.

8. Chen, Shengkai, Shuliang Fang, and Renzhong Tang. "An ANN-based approach for real-time scheduling in cloud manufacturing." *Applied Sciences* 10, no. 7 (2020): 2491.

9. Hasan, Md, Md Almamun, and Shawkat Akbar. "An intelligent machine learning and self adaptive resource allocation framework for cloud computing environment." *EAI Endorsed Transactions on Cloud Systems* 6, no. 18 (2020).

10. Kholidy, Hisham A. "An intelligent swarm based prediction approach for predicting cloud computing user resource needs." *Computer Communications* 151 (2020): 133–144.

CHAPTER 6

Machine Learning-Based Predictive Model to Improve Cloud Application Performance in Cloud SaaS

Falguni Sharma and Punit Gupta

CONTENTS

6.1 INTRODUCTION

The term cloud refers to a huge network or space on the web. It is an innovation that utilizes distant workers on the web to store, develop, deploy, maintain and access information online rather than using local drives or machines. The information can be anything, for example, records, pictures, reports, sound, video, and the sky's the limit. Small or huge, all IT

DOI: 10.1201/9781003185376-6

organizations follow the conventional techniques with regard to IT infrastructure. All IT organizations need a server room which is a considerably essential need of an organization. A server room consists of a database server, mail server, network, switches, firewalls, modem, switches, a query per second (QPS) method which deals with the load of queries a server can resolve in a given time, framework, high-speed Internet and maintenance and support engineers. A lot of economic support is needed to set up such infrastructure in an organization and maintain it at same time. To resolve the issues of traditional IT infrastructure and to decrease the IT infrastructure cost, the cloud computing approach was invented by innovators (Figure 6.1).

Cloud computing technology provides infrastructure such as virtual machines, servers, data centers; platforms for the development and deployment of software; and applications to users over the Internet. Cloud provides deployment models and service models on which all workings of cloud depend. There are four types of deployment models used in the cloud framework: Public cloud, private cloud, community cloud and hybrid cloud. Deployment models are defined on the basis of where the cloud infrastructure for the environment is located. All the services in

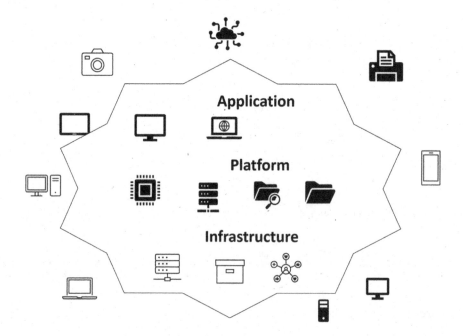

FIGURE 6.1   Cloud architecture.

cloud have been categorized into three service models according to their service type.

The service models of cloud are infrastructure-as-a-service (IaaS) which provides virtualized computational resources, platform-as-a-service (PaaS) which offers platforms to developers to develop a framework which can be easily built and run and software-as-a-service (SaaS) which provides licensed applications and software on subscription or free to use for cloud users (Figure 6.2). In PaaS the developer doesn't need infrastructure to run or create the application; resources and APIs can be called as needed.

Machine learning is the extended application area of artificial intelligence which facilitates automatic learning in systems without being explicitly programmed. The difference between artificial intelligence and machine learning is that artificial intelligence completes the task in a smart way while machine learning provides data to machines to learn themselves. The extended version of machine learning is deep learning which mimics human brain activities using neural networks and other approaches in object detection, object recognition, speech recognition, language translation and making decisions. Machine learning is further

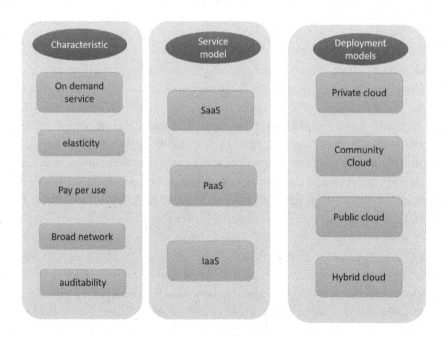

FIGURE 6.2   Cloud service models and deployment models.

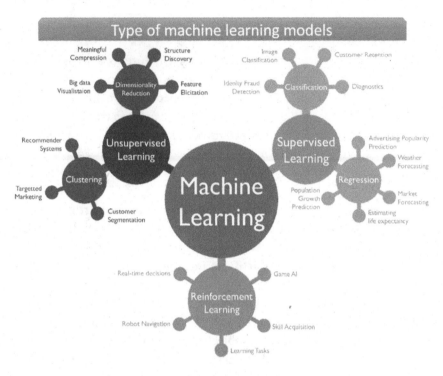

FIGURE 6.3 Machine learning approaches in cloud.

divided into three parts: Supervised, unsupervised and reinforcement, as observed by Dey (2016) in *machine learning algorithms* [10] (Figure 6.3).

Predictive models in machine learning are the models which are able to predict happenings before time using past available data or present data. Neural networks, logistic regression, random forests and decision trees are some of the machine learning predictive models applied in cloud applications to improve the performance of existing systems; for example decision fusion techniques and structural risk minimization are used for resource availability prediction in cloud applications as stated by Nikravesh et al. (2017) in *autonomic prediction suite* [11] (Figure 6.4).

Cloud computing works in various areas such as multi-cloud strategies, hyperscale data centers, cloud security, cloud backup and retrieval, cloud-based network services and serverless architecture. Cloud applications are the software or applications which are deployed or developed in a cloud environment rather than hosted on a local environment or machine. To improve the cloud applications performance there are

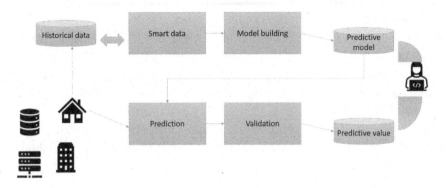

FIGURE 6.4 Working of a prediction model.

FIGURE 6.5 Cloud performance indices.

numerous algorithms developed by researchers over time. In this chapter we are going to discuss such algorithms and their results in comparison with existing frameworks (Figure 6.5).

Return on investment (ROI) is a performance measure. ROI is used to evaluate or compare the efficiency of investment. ROI includes cloud computing ROI models to efficiently complete this task as stated in *ROI from cloud computing* (Skilton, 2010, p.22) [12]; to evaluate the performance of cloud applications in SaaS there are key performance indices (KPIs). KPIs target cloud computing comparison with traditional IT and cloud computing solutions. The main KPIs in the cloud are time, cost, quality and profitability or margin as stated by Lin (2013) in *performance indicator evaluation* [13]. In this paper we will discuss three cloud KPIs: Time, cost and quality.

Three models of time KPIs play a crucial role in deciding the performance of an application in SaaS: Average response time, maximum response time, response time failure. All three are service response time types. The average response time should be minimum to provide enhanced performance for cloud applications in SaaS. The next KPI is cost. Cost depends on two factors: Acquisition and ongoing. It is a challenge for cloud providers to rate services on providing different features for one service. The same cloud service provider may provide different VMs which satisfy different user needs. The last KPI is quality. The quality of cloud services depends on four attributes: Correlation, practicality and computability, consistency and discriminative power. Each attribute plays a vital role in cloud elasticity, accuracy, transparency, suitability, reliability, availability, throughput and efficiency as stated by Garg (2013) in *future generation computer systems* [14].

According to the definition of NIST there are five essential characteristics of cloud models, three service models and four deployment models; all are explained as follows.

6.1.1 Essential Characteristics

According to the NIST definition here are the five essential characteristics of cloud:

- On-demand self-service.

- Broad network access.

- Resource pooling.

- Rapid elasticity.

- Measured service.

Source: Based on 'The NIST Definition of Cloud Computing', Special Publication 800-145, NIST, US [21].

6.1.2 Cloud Delivery/Deployment Model

As per the NIST definition, cloud models are divided into four models [21] (Figure 6.6):

a) **Public cloud**: A public cloud is offered by third-party providers. It is accessible for all through the Internet. A public cloud scales quickly and is convenient for all to access. Maintenance is taken care of by the service provider. Resources are shared which causes less security,

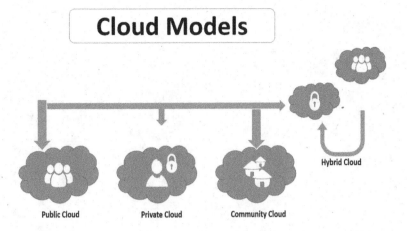

FIGURE 6.6   Cloud deployment models.

flexibility and control over the cloud environment. Examples are Amazon EC2 andGoogle App Engine.

b) **Private cloud**: As the name indicates, this is a dedicated cloud service where resources are exclusively used by a single entity or an organization. It provides high security as resources are not shared. High flexibility to control the cloud environment. It is more expensive than public cloud as services and maintenance have to be taken care of by the organization. Examples are VMware, Microsoft, KVM and Xen.

c) **Hybrid cloud**: This is also known as the best of both worlds. It combines the best features of public and private cloud. Greater flexibility, high security, more features, more deployment options and cloud bursting are also possible. It is expensive, and the network is complex. Examples are IBM, HP, Vmware, vCloud, and eucalyptus.

d) **Community cloud**: Different types of cloud are integrated to solve a mutual purpose. A community cloud provides high security, reliability and performance. Its scalability is limited, and it is high in cost. Examples are SolaS and VMware.

6.1.3 Cloud Service/Model Type

There are three cloud services defined by Mell (2011) in *NIST definition of cloud computing* [21]. Those are IaaS, PaaS and SaaS, focused on hardware, system software and application respectively (Figure 6.7).

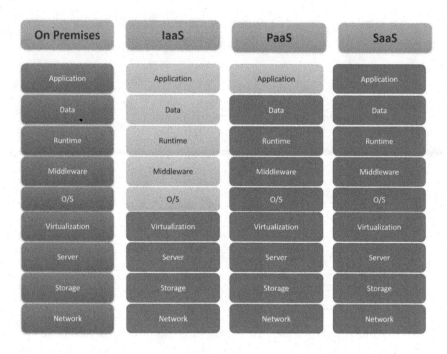

FIGURE 6.7   Cloud services control comparison.

a) **Software as a service (SaaS)**: This service provides software applications over the Internet on demand. Users need not install this
on their local machines. The software can be accessed by the user
through a web browser. The application cannot be controlled by the
user; it can only be used. All the maintenance and updates are handled by the provider.

b) **Platform as a service (PaaS)**: This refers to the cloud administration
which provides the environment to create, test, develop and deploy the
product applications. Clients can introduce and control the applications
on the given stage. PaaS incorporates administrations like server, database, systems administration and development tools.

c) **Infrastructure as a service (IaaS)**: IaaS gives the entire framework
as a service, it can rapidly scale all over on internet and you pay for
what you use. Users can purchase, install, configure and manage
their own product, application and software, operating system and
any application, while the infrastructure is managed by the service
provider.

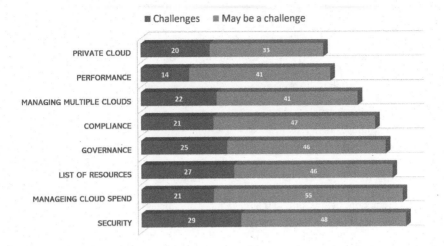

■ Challenges   ■ May be a challenge

PRIVATE CLOUD	20	33
PERFORMANCE	14	41
MANAGING MULTIPLE CLOUDS	22	41
COMPLIANCE	21	47
GOVERNANCE	25	46
LIST OF RESOURCES	27	46
MANAGEING CLOUD SPEND	21	55
SECURITY	29	48

FIGURE 6.8   Cloud challenges.

6.2 CLOUD CHALLENGES

Cloud is a standalone technology to manage resources and the processing and overseeing of information. There are challenges and difficulties to maintain transparency, consistency of cloud is likewise expanding. The cloud may deal with issues like resource optimization, scaling, security, maintenance and others.

In Figure 6.8 a survey by Rightscale (2018) shows the cloud challenges. It is clearly visible that security in the cloud has significant challenges following the other challenges in the field of cloud computing. To enhance the working of the cloud all these challenges should be overcome with better solutions.

6.3 LITERATURE REVIEW

Content
[1]   Raza et al. (2019) presented a machine learning model for comparative analysis in which they discussed 11 machine learning classification approaches. In one of the machine learning approaches, the Friedman test and Nemenyi's post hoc test are applied to identify the difference among the classifiers performance during ten-fold cross validation on the training dataset to identify the best parameters for all machine learning approaches to get the optimal solution. SaaS is an application-based service among other cloud applications.

(Continued)

	Content
[2]	Ahmed et al. (2018) presented a model to improve the performance of virtual machines using an optimization model using parallel particle swarm optimization. In this approach they discussed linear regression and neural network machine learning approaches to achieve improved performance of VMs. As a result they observed that the proposed model provided a result 64% better than existing models for chronic kidney diseases for cloud computing-based high computing system (HCS).
[3]	Kirchoff et al. (2019) presented supervised machine learning workload prediction techniques in which they compared three machine learning approaches, ARIMA, MLP and GRU, under various cloud environments and configurations. The obtained results show that all three approaches are good for short-term predictions. ARIMA needs a large number of samples to compute optimal results. ARIMA is time consuming. GRU achieved the best results among the three in terms of flexibility of use, sensitivity to the number of samples, execution time and accuracy.
[4]	In [4] Esfahani et al. (2015), the authors proposed a knowledge-based adaptable scheduler to minimize SLA violation and maximize the profit using customized decision tree algorithms for resource allocation. The proposed method obtained 38.4% cost savings compared to previous research work.
[6]	Borkowski et al. (2016) [6] presented an approach for predicting cloud resource utilization performance improvement model using an ANN backpropagation machine learning prediction model. The prediction model was built using historical data and a real world dataset. We evaluated the approach and the result shows that it increased accuracy, compared to a simple regression approach. The results showed that this approach reduced prediction error by 20% for median cases, and 89% less prediction error has been obtained for the best cases using the proposed model.
[7]	Alkalbani et al. (2016) introduced five supervised machine learning prediction approaches in [7] to predict the sentiments of SaaS online customer reviews. The result shows a 92.37% accuracy rate has been obtained using the space vector five-fold cross validation approach. This approach worked best compared with other models.
[8]	Tripathy et al. (2020) in [8] proposed an SQL injection attacks detection approach using machine learning classifiers for SaaS. The proposed method obtained a 99.3% accuracy detection rate using five features and a 99.4% accuracy detection rate using seven features with AdaBoostClassifier.
[15]	Sharkh et al. (2020) introduced a new cloud performance prediction technique using TU Delft Bitbrains traces dataset by applying machine learning approaches on the dataset. Any improvement on prediction has a direct effect on KPI for both cloud clients and providers. The linear regression approach produces optimum results for mean absolute percentage error disk write throughput. The support vector machine (SVM) learning approach produced optimum results for root mean squared error, network received throughput and network transmitted throughput to improve cloud resource scheduling in a cloud data center.

(Continued)

	Content
[17]	Pandita et al. (2020) proposed a neural network machine learning fault predicting model approach. A Bayesian regularized artificial neural network approach was used to predict application performance and the results obtained by the proposed model were 97.6% for a Google Cloud selected dataset.
[18]	Govindraju et al. (2020) proposed a regression tree model to obtain the performance accuracy of virtual machine startup time. An OpenStack test environment was used to calculate the efficiency of the proposed model. The proposed model predicted virtual machines' startup times with an average accuracy rate of 91.81%.
[19]	Shetty et al. (2020) in [19] proposed a supervised machine learning predictive approach for healthcare data in cloud environments which focused on two areas. First, analysis of the algorithms in the field of healthcare. Prediction models are tested on the performance metrics such as accuracy, precision, f1 score and recall. Results obtained by the calculations showed that the random forest prediction model obtained best results among other supervised machine learning approaches.
[20]	Sergue (2020) in [20] presented a machine learning prediction model with linear regression and random forest approaches for an SaaS cloud service model. A nonlinear random forest regression technique obtained better results than a linear regression technique for particular scenarios.
[22]	Madni et al. (2020) proposed a fuzzy cuckoo search technique based on the fuzzy theory and cuckoo search to solve real-time optimization problems. In IaaS cloud FCS addresses reliability-aware resource scheduling problems. The FCS technique was compared with genetic algorithms (GA), honey bee (HB) and PSO. The result shows FCS produced 39.21% better results than GA, HB and PSO in terms of failure rate.
[23]	Chen et al. (2020) proposed a self-adaptive resource allocation method using a QoS prediction model and PSO runtime decision algo model. The proposed method produced 15% better results using the same historical data. The effectiveness of cloud application resource allocation was improved by around 5–6%.
[24]	Shahidinejad et al. (2020) proposed a framework which used learning automata as a decision maker to offload the incoming dynamic workloads onto the cloud servers. Another approach proposed an edge server provisioning approach using a long short-term memory model to estimate the future workload and reinforcement learning technique to make an appropriate scaling decision. Results show the proposed framework increases the CPU utilization and reduces the execution time and energy consumption.
[25]	Hasan et al. (2020) proposed a self-adaptive resource allocation framework based on machine learning to resolve issues in multi-dimensional cloud resources. The authors compared QoS prediction model, improved bat algorithm (IBA), energy-efficient model (EEM), modified colonel selection algorithm (MCSA) and enhanced recurrent neural network (ERNN) machine learning approaches for a resource allocation framework.

(Continued)

	Content
[16]	Morariu et al. (2020) proposed predictive production planning and predictive maintenance for operation scheduling and resource allocation in cloud environments. The authors introduced AI-based approaches for reality awareness and resources optimization in cloud production. The proposed approach also provides optimal results for the prediction of energy consumption patterns.
[26]	Mazidi et al. (2020) proposed an approach using MAPE-K loop and hybrid resource load prediction for the automatic scalability of resources for multilayered cloud applications to predict resource demand in future. The results obtained using a cloud simulator indicate the enhancement of the proposed framework in terms of operational cost, the resources used and the amount of profit.
[27]	Mazidi et al. (2020) proposed a KNN-based machine learning approach using a MAPE-K loop to autoscale the resources for multilayered cloud applications. The result shows the proposed framework reduced operational cost and improved resource utilization, response time and profit.
[28]	Osypanka et al. (2020) proposed a framework which uses an anomaly-detection machine learning PSO approach to achieve optimal cost resource configuration. The result was tested in a Microsoft Azure environment which shows 85% cost reduction in ten months using real-time data.
[29]	Kaur et al. (2021) proposed an optimized prediction scheduling approach which combines the features of TOPSIS and swarm intelligence using optimal virtual machines. The proposed framework minimizes cost, execution time and SLA violation and improves resource allocation optimization and reliability.
[30]	Rawat et al. (2021) proposed a machine learning algorithm to improve the performance of applications in SaaS cloud by deploying a cloud-based service architecture for managing machine learning models which are best fit for the Internet of things security parameters in an SaaS cloud environment.
[31]	Rangra et al. (2021) proposed a framework for big data storage in cloud mechanics to enhance the performance in terms of cost, time and accuracy of mobile digital healthcare SaaS applications. The authors proposed a deep learning approach to resolve the issues in digital healthcare which involves the step of computing in the cloud server in optimized format.
[32]	Jha et al. (2021) proposed a framework to improve the performance of SaaS applications in cloud environments by applying machine learning models. The authors worked on huge live datasets to get optimum results using machine learning approaches.
[33]	Paramsivapandi et al. (2021) proposed a machine learning framework to find an error-free solution for data reading and writing during SaaS application access. The proposed framework, a hybrid recurrent data-driven flow algorithm (HRD-DFA), proposes an optimum solution for reduced error during application access.

TABLE 6.1   A Extensive Study of Various Models for Optimization in Cloud

	Authors	Approach	Result/Conclusion
[1]	Raza et al. (2019)	K-NN, naive Bayes, logistic regression, Rocchio, perceptron, Ridge, SGD, decision tree, SVM, passive aggressive, logistic regression prediction models used.	Logistic regression highest performance obtained in the proposed scenario.
[2]	Ahmed et al. (2018)	Linear regression, neural network, cloud, performance of VMs, model for chronic kidney diagnosis and prediction, VMs performance optimization model for cloud computing-based HCS using parallel particle swarm optimization (PPSO).	50% improved performance in execution time. Real-time data retrieval system efficiency 5.2% improved. Accuracy of hybrid model in prediction of CKD 97.8%. Overall performance is 64% better than existing models for the same.
[3]	Kirchoff et al. (2019)	ARIMA, MLP, GRU, cloud, maintaining QoS, avoiding SLA, hyperparameters are used as samples.	All three techniques are good for short-term predictions. ARIMA needs more samples, needs to update, needs to recalculate for each series and is time consuming. GRU achieved the best results among the three in terms of flexibility of use, execution time, sensitivity to the number of samples and accuracy.
[4]	Esfahani et al. (2015)	Decision tree, deadline, budget, length, penalty rate.	Reduced SLA violation, results obtained through simulation show that proposed algorithm provides significant improvement of up to 38.4% cost saving.
[6]	Borkowski et al. (2016)	ANN, backpropagation, multiple linear regression approaches applied on dataset of travis, Cl, GitHub to obtain cloud resource allocation prediction on per task and per resource level performance analysis.	Proposed model reduced the prediction error by 20% in the typical case with improvements above 89% among the best cases.

(Continued)

TABLE 6.1 (CONTINUED)   A Extensive Study of Various Models for Optimization in Cloud

	Authors	Approach	Result/Conclusion
[7]	**Alkalbani et al. (2016)**	SVM, naive Bayes, naive Bayes (kernel), KNN, decision tree, SaaS polarity dataset, space vector algorithm five-fold cross validation, accuracy, classification, precision.	92.37% accuracy rate, using space vector five-fold cross validation approach.
[8]	**Tripathy et al. (2020)**	Random forest classifier, deep ANN, decision tree, Tensorflow's linear classifier, Adaboost classifier, optimized linear classifier, boosted trees classifier, detecting SQL injection attacks in cloud SaaS using machine learning models.	Random forest classifier outperforms all others on the dataset and achieves 99.8% accuracy.
[15]	**Sharkh et al. (2020)**	Linear regression, SVM, random forest, REP tree, deep learning, TU Delft Bitbrains traces.	Design a cloud application behavior prediction technique based on machine learning predictors, optimum results obtained using linear regression and SVM.
[17]	**Pandita et al. (2020)**	Bayesian regularized artificial neural network, Google cloud, parameters: Bandwidth, disk and memory.	It has been seen that the Bayesian regularized NN algorithm, which is an expansion of the backpropagation approach, gives the best results for small datasets. It resolves overfitting issues and assembles the most summed up model which can be utilized with unwavering quality. BRANN indicated an awesome execution precision of 96.4% and 97.6% for DS1 and DS2, separately.
[18]	**Govindraju et al. (2020)**	Regression tree, VM resource allocation OpenStack test environment, VM startup prediction average, min, max.	Model predicted average accuracy 91.81% for VM startup.

(Continued)

TABLE 6.1 (CONTINUED)   A Extensive Study of Various Models for Optimization in Cloud

	Authors	Approach	Result/Conclusion
[19]	Shetty et al. (2020)	Naive Bayes, decision trees, random forest, linear regression, performance metrics such as accuracy precision f1 score and recall.	Random forest obtained best results.
[20]	Sergue (2020)	Logistic regression, random forest, customer phone dataset, oversampling, under sampling, time series cross validation.	Random forest obtained better performance than logistic regression.
[22]	Madni et al. (2020)	Fuzzy cuckoo search technique, fuzzy theory, cuckoo search algorithm which solves real-time optimization problematic issue, FCS addresses reliability-aware resource scheduling problems in IaaS cloud.	FCS obtained 39.21% better optimal solutions. FCS technique is more appropriate for reliability-aware resource scheduling for IaaS cloud.
[23]	Chen et al. (2020)	QoS prediction model and PSO-based runtime decision algorithm.	15% better results than existing algorithms. The effectiveness of cloud application resource allocation has been improved by around 5–6%.
[24]	Shahidinejad et al. (2020)	Learning automata as decision maker to offload the incoming dynamic workloads into the edge or cloud servers.	Proposed framework increases CPU utilization, reduces execution time, reduces energy consumption.
[25]	Hasan et al. (2020)	QoS prediction model, improved bat algorithm, energy-efficient model, modified colonel selection algorithm, enhanced recurrent neural network.	QoS prediction model enhances accuracy, MCSA minimizes the energy depletion, speedy resource allocation by enhanced RNN.
[16]	Morariu et al. (2020)	Long short-term memory neural networks, deep learning in real time to re-assign resources, detect anomalies.	Information stored in logical streams, NN trained to find possible anomalies or variations relative to the normal patterns of energy consumption at each layer.

(Continued)

TABLE 6.1 (CONTINUED)   A Extensive Study of Various Models for Optimization in Cloud

	Authors	Approach	Result/Conclusion
[26]	**Mazidi et al. (2020)**	MAPE-K loop, Google penalty payment model, hybrid resource load prediction algorithm, statistical solution, risk-aware algorithm.	Operational costs decreased, optimum use of resources, cost effectiveness.
[27]	**Mazidi et al. (2020)**	K-NN to analyze and label VMs, MAPE-K loop to autoscale the resources for multilayered cloud applications.	Operational cost reduction, optimal resource utilization, response time and profit.
[28]	**Osypanka et al. (2020)**	Anomaly detection, machine learning and PSO.	In ten months' observation in Microsoft Azure environment 85% cost reduction successfully obtained by given approach.
[29]	**Kaur et al. (2021)**	Optimized prediction scheduling approach, scientific application with optimal VM by combining the features of swarm intelligence and TOPSIS.	Obtained results using given approach shows minimizing the execution time, cost, SLA violation rate.
[30]	**Rawat et al. (2021)**	Random forest classifier (RFC) used for feature selection; 15 features were selected for investigation. Five machine learning models, naive Bayes, decision tree, logistic regression, KNN and DNN, applied to generate optimum results.	Obtained result shows best working model naive Bayes, followed by DT and LR. KNN and DNN are impractical to use in IoT devices from the operational perspective.
[31]	**Rangra et al. (2021)**	Improving the performance of big data storage on cloud mechanics using deep learning approaches which overall improves SaaS application's performance and reliability.	Obtained result shows the overall improvement in performance metrics cost, time and accuracy.

(Continued)

TABLE 6.1 (CONTINUED)   A Extensive Study of Various Models for Optimization in Cloud

	Authors	Approach	Result/Conclusion
[32]	**Jha et al. (2021)**	Predictive models such as SVM, decision tree, naive Bayes, random forest, KNN and logistic regression applied and compared against the optimum results to predict the customers' behavior.	Obtained result shows the enhancement in cloud applications' reliability, quality and performance.
[33]	**Paramsiva-pandi et al. (2021)**	HRD-DFA is proposed to monitor the cloud's data flow error. It generates system check during the reading writing process.	Obtained result shows that proposed framework reduced error in data stream during read write process.

See also Table 6.1.

6.4 COMPARATIVE ANALYSIS

See Table 6.2.

6.5 CONCLUSION

Cloud computing technology is increasingly widespread in the enterprise and business markets. An effective resource allocation algorithm is required using machine learning predictive models to improve cloud applications dedicatedly for SaaS cloud service models. This paper summarizes the resource allocation and optimization techniques using machine learning predictive models and their impacts in cloud environments. Some of the strategies discussed in this paper are focused on cloud optimization but lacking in fault awareness techniques. Hence this survey paper motivates future researchers to come up with smarter fault-aware and cloud reliable frameworks for cloud systems.

TABLE 6.2 Literature Review Comparative Analysis of Prediction Models for Resource Optimization Using Various Performance Metrics

S. No.	Author	Proposed Algo.	Focused on			
			Reliability	Resource Optimization	Quality	Other Parameters
[1]	Raza et al. (2019)	Quality pillar assessment of SaaS services	✓	–	✓	–
[2]	Ahmed et al. (2018)	Parallel particle swarm optimization algorithm to optimize VM selection	✓	✓	–	–
[3]	Kirchoff et al. (2019)	ARIMA, MLP and GRU workload prediction technique	✓	✓	–	–
[4]	Esfahani et al. (2015)	Knowledge-based admission control with scheduling algorithm	✓	✓	✓	–
[6]	Borkowski et al. (2016)	Predicting cloud resource utilization on per task and per resource level	✓	✓	–	–
[7]	Alkalbani et al. (2016)	Develop prediction models to predict the sentiment of SaaS consumers' reviews	✓	–	✓	–
[8]	Tripathy et al. (2020)	Investigate the potential of using machine learning techniques for SQL injection detection on the application level	✓	–	–	Security
[15]	Sharkh et al. (2020)	Cloud computing application performance improvement through machine learning	✓	✓	✓	–
[17]	Pandita et al. (2020)	SLA violation in cloud computing using BRANN	✓	–	✓	–
[18]	Govindraju et al. (2020)	Regression tree predictive model for virtual machine startup time in IaaS clouds	✓	✓	–	–

(Continued)

TABLE 6.2 (Continued) Literature Review Comparative Analysis of Prediction Models for Resource Optimization Using Various Performance Metrics

S. No.	Author	Proposed Algo.	Reliability	Focused on			Other Parameters
				Resource Optimization	Quality		
[19]	Shetty et al. (2020)	Predictive algorithms for healthcare data in cloud environment	✓	–	–		Performance metric: Accuracy, precision, f1 score, recall
[20]	Sergue (2020)	Churn analysis and prediction using machine learning for a B2B SaaS company	✓	–	–		Performance
[22]	Madni et al. (2020)	Reliability-aware resource scheduling based on fuzzy cuckoo search technique for IaaS	✓	–	–		–
[23]	Chen et al. (2020)	Iterative QoS prediction model PSO based runtime decision making algorithm adaptive resource allocation framework	✓	–	✓		–
[24]	Shahidinejad et al. (2020)	Joint computation offloading and resource provisioning for edge cloud computing environment	✓	✓	✓		–
[25]	Hasan et al. (2020)	Self-adaptive resource allocation framework based on machine learning is proposed for modeling and analyzing the problem of multi-dimensional cloud resource	✓	✓	✓		Energy depletion
[16]	Morariu et al. (2020)	Long short-term memory neural networks and deep learning in real time to re-assign resources	✓	✓	✓		Energy consumption, anomaly detection, cost optimization

(Continued)

TABLE 6.2 (Continued) Literature Review Comparative Analysis of Prediction Models for Resource Optimization Using Various Performance Metrics

S. No.	Author	Proposed Algo.	Focused on			Other Parameters
			Reliability	Resource Optimization	Quality	
[26]	Mazidi et al. (2020)	Solution to automatic scalability of resources for multilayered cloud applications under the monitor analysis plan execute knowledge loop	✓	✓	✓	Penalty costs
[27]	Mazidi et al. (2020)	MAPE-K loop to autoscale the resources for multilayered cloud applications resource allocation algorithm	✓	✓	✓	Operational costs, response time
[28]	Osypanka et al. (2020)	Anomaly detection machine learning and particle swarm optimization to achieve a cost optimal cloud resource configuration	✓	✓	✓	Cost optimization, anomaly detection
[29]	Kaur et al. (2021)	Resource allocation for scientific applications in a virtualized cloud environment	✓	✓	✓	Cost
[30]	Rawat et al. (2021)	Cloud-assisted ML-based security solution, proposed cloud-based service architecture for ML model management to generate optimum security results for IoT devices	✓	-	-	Security
[31]	Rangra et al. (2021)	Deep learning approaches to improve SaaS application's performance metrics and reliability	✓	-	✓	Cost, time, accuracy
[32]	Jha et al. (2021)	Predicting users' behavior using machine learning models	✓	-	✓	-
[33]	Paramsivapandi et al. (2021)	Reducing error during data streaming in SaaS applications	✓	-	✓	-

REFERENCES

1. Raza, M., Hussain, F. K., Hussain, O. K., Zhao et al. (2019). A comparative analysis of machine learning models for quality pillar assessment of SaaS services by multi-class text classification of users' reviews. *Future Generation Computer Systems, 101,* 341–371.
2. Abdelaziz, A., Elhoseny, M., Salama, A. S., & Riad, A. M. (2018). A machine learning model for improving healthcare services in cloud computing environments. *Measurement, 119,* 117–128.
3. Kirchoff, D. F., Xavier, M., Mastella, J., & De Rose, C. A. (2019, February). A preliminary study of machine learning workload prediction techniques for cloud applications. In 2019 27th Euromicro International Conference on Parallel, Distributed and Network-Based Processing (PDP) (pp. 222–227). IEEE.
4. Motavaselalhagh, F., Esfahani, F. S., & Arabnia, H. R. (2015). Knowledge-based adaptable scheduler for SaaS providers in cloud computing. *Human-centric Computing and Information Sciences, 5*(1), 1–19.
5. Pop, D. (2016). Machine learning and cloud computing: Survey of distributed and saas solutions. IEAT Technical Report, pp. 1–12 (2012). arXiv preprint arXiv:1603.08767.
6. Borkowski, M., Schulte, S., & Hochreiner, C. (2016, December). Predicting cloud resource utilization. In Proceedings of the 9th International Conference on Utility and Cloud Computing (pp. 37–42).
7. Alkalbani, A. M., Ghamry, A. M., Hussain, F. K., & Hussain, O. K. (2016, July). Predicting the sentiment of SaaS online reviews using supervised machine learning techniques. In 2016 International Joint Conference on Neural Networks (IJCNN) (pp. 1547–1553). IEEE.
8. Tripathy, D., Gohil, R., & Halabi, T. (2020, May). Detecting SQL injection attacks in cloud SaaS using machine learning. In 2020 IEEE 6th International Conference on Big Data Security on Cloud (BigDataSecurity), IEEE Intl Conference on High Performance and Smart Computing,(HPSC) and IEEE Intl Conference on Intelligent Data and Security (IDS) (pp. 145–150). IEEE.
9. Duvvuri, V. (2020). Minerva: A portable machine learning microservice framework for traditional enterprise SaaS applications. arXiv preprint arXiv:2005.00866.
10. Dey, A. (2016). Machine learning algorithms: A review. *International Journal of Computer Science and Information Technologies, 7*(3), 1174–1179.
11. Nikravesh, A. Y., Ajila, S. A., & Lung, C. H. (2017). An autonomic prediction suite for cloud resource provisioning. *Journal of Cloud Computing, 6*(1), 1–20.
12. Skilton, M., & Director, C. (2010). Building return on investment from cloud computing. In *White Paper.* The Open Group.
13. Lin, Y. K., & Chang, P. C. (2013). Performance indicator evaluation for a cloud computing system from QoS viewpoint. *Quality & Quantity, 47*(3), 1605–1616.

14. Garg, S. K., Versteeg, S., & Buyya, R. (2013). A framework for ranking of cloud computing services. *Future Generation Computer Systems, 29*(4), 1012–1023.

15. Sharkh, M. A., Xu, Y., & Leyder, E. CloudMach: Cloud computing application performance improvement through machine learning. In 2020 IEEE Canadian Conference on Electrical and Computer Engineering (CCECE) (pp. 1–6). IEEE.

16. Morariu, C., Morariu, O., Răileanu, S., & Borangiu, T. (2020). Machine learning for predictive scheduling and resource allocation in large scale manufacturing systems. *Computers in Industry, 120*, 103244.

17. Pandita, A., Upadhyay, P. K., & Joshi, N. (2020, February). Prediction of service-level agreement violation in Cloud computing using bayesian regularisation. In International Conference on Advanced Machine Learning Technologies and Applications (pp. 231–242). Springer.

18. Govindaraju, Y., Duran-Limon, H. A., & Mezura-Montes, E. (2020). A regression tree predictive model for virtual machine startup time in IaaS clouds. *Cluster Computing, 24*(2), 1–17.

19. Shetty, S. K., & Patil, A. P. (2020, July). Implementation and analysis of predictive algorithms for healthcare data in cloud environment. In 2020 IEEE International Conference on Electronics, Computing and Communication Technologies (CONECCT) (pp. 1–6). IEEE.

20. Sergue, M. (2020). Customer churn analysis and prediction using machine learning for a B2B SaaS company.

21. Mell, P., & Grance, T. (2011). *The NIST Definition of Cloud Computing. Institute of Science and Technology, Special Publication, 800*, 145.

22. Madni, S. H. H., Abd Latiff, M. S., & Abdullah, A. H. (2020, July). Reliability aware resource scheduling based on fuzzy cuckoo search (FCS) technique for IaaS cloud. In *IOP Conference Series: Materials Science and Engineering* (Vol. 884, No. 1, p. 012053). IOP Publishing.

23. Chen, X., Wang, H., Ma, Y., Zheng, X., & Guo, L. (2020). Self-adaptive resource allocation for cloud-based software services based on iterative QoS prediction model. *Future Generation Computer Systems, 105*, 287–296.

24. Shahidinejad, A., & Ghobaei-Arani, M. (2020). Joint computation offloading and resource provisioning for e dge-cloud computing environment: A machine learning-based approach. Software: *Practice and Experience, 50*(12), 2212–2230.

25. Hasan, M., Almamun, M., & Akbar, S. (2020). An intelligent machine learning and self adaptive resource allocation framework for cloud computing environment. *EAI Endorsed Transactions on Cloud Systems, 6*(18), 5–9.

26. Mazidi, A., Golsorkhtabaramiri, M., & Yadollahzadeh Tabari, M. (2020). An autonomic risk-and penalty-aware resource allocation with probabilistic resource scaling mechanism for multilayer cloud resource provisioning. *International Journal of Communication Systems, 33*(7), e4334.

27. Mazidi, A., Golsorkhtabaramiri, M., & Tabari, M. Y. (2020). Autonomic resource provisioning for multilayer cloud applications with K-nearest neighbor resource scaling and priority-based resource allocation. *Software: Practice and Experience*, *50*(8), 1600–1625.

28. Osypanka, P., & Nawrocki, P. (2020). Resource usage cost optimization in cloud computing using machine learning. *IEEE Transactions on Cloud Computing*.

29. Kaur, G., & Bala, A. (2021). OPSA: An optimized prediction based scheduling approach for scientific applications in cloud environments. *Cluster Computing*, *24*, 1955–1974.

30. Alsharif, M., & Rawat, D. B. (2021). Study of machine learning for cloud assisted iot security as a service. *Sensors*, *21*(4), 1034.

31. Rangra, A., & Sehgal, V. K. (2021). On performance of big data storage on cloud mechanics in mobile digital healthcare. *International Journal of E-Health and Medical Communications (IJEHMC)*, *12*(5), 36–49.

32. Jha, P., & Sharma, A. (2021, January). Framework to analyze malicious behaviour in cloud environment using machine learning techniques. In *2021 International Conference on Computer Communication and Informatics (ICCCI)* (pp. 1–12). IEEE.

33. Paramsivapandi, M. S. K., & Nagarajan, S. (2021). Machine learning based hybrid recurrent data-driven flow algorithm of identify the risk of data flow error detection in cloud computing. *International Journal for Research in Applied Science & Engineering Technology*, *9*(2).

CHAPTER 7

Fault-Aware Machine Learning and Deep Learning-Based Algorithm for Cloud Architecture

Deepika Agarwal, Sneha Agrawal and Punit Gupta

CONTENTS

DOI: 10.1201/9781003185376-7

7.1 INTRODUCTION

The reliability of the system is measured using the failure probability of the system [4]. In this article, we introduce a proactive, predictive power-aware fault-tolerant efficient scheduling technique which is based on a hybrid approach using a bat algorithm and feedforward neural network [1]. This is also known as fault-tolerant power-efficient ANN-based scheduling (FTS-ANN). Results demonstrate that the proposed bat-ANN technique improves the reliability of the virtual machines. The paper is organized as follows. Section 7.2 presents a brief literature review focusing on fault-tolerant scheduling in the cloud. Section 7.3 illustrates the proposed FTS-ANN technique. Section 7.4 presents the experimental results of FTS-ANN compared with the other static, dynamic and meta-heuristics techniques based on a proactive fault-tolerant aware scheduling mechanism. It also covers the detailed discussions of the outcomes using the FTS-ANN model. Finally, Section 7.5 covers the conclusions and future extension of the work.

7.2 RELATED WORK

The authors Charity et al. presented a technique for increasing the reliability of storage, computing and network resources [2]. The system setup measures the trust level of each virtual machine and then allocates the cloudlets on a more trusted virtual machine. The presented technique provides a stable and reliable allocation of the virtual machine [3]. There is a limitation in that the authors only focused on a proactive approach. The reactive techniques are not explored. Zhou et al. considered the reliability of the cloud services which include infrastructure, platform and application as a service. The authors focused on virtual machine allocation on the host using data center network topology and a K-fault tolerance guarantee using the key features of graph theory in a cloud environment. The authors considered the cloudlet's allocation reliable virtual machine [7]. The reliability will improve further focusing on tasks to virtual machine allocation.

A Monte Carlo failure measurement technique was tested to probe the future trends of cloudlets allocation. The chance of the fault at virtual machines hosted on the data center is estimated using probabilistic

Weibull failure distribution based on randomness feature. Rehani et al. proposed the cloudlet allocation on a reliable virtual machine; a failure-aware resource reservation technique is presented which uses the reliability as a benchmark test parameter [5, 6].

The authors presented a system of fault tolerance-aware scheduling which reduces the scheduled time because the virtual machine with a higher trust level is allocated for the cloudlet scheduling [8]. Hence the researchers observed that reliability is still a challenging issue. The presented work will be helpful for us to propose a robust model having a higher level of significance and level of trust. The scheduling issue in the cloud comes under the category of the NP-hard problem. Hence this prominent issue is solved using nature-inspired heuristic and meta-heuristic techniques for reliable allocation in large populations. The selection of heuristic-based techniques relies on problem statement Heuristic algorithm is developed to maximize the reliability of cloud services for end-users across the globe [7].

The accuracy is measured under reliability threshold values for the allocation of the cloudlets on virtual machines. Resource allocation techniques differ from the centralized techniques where the primary host makes the decision; in nature-inspired heuristic approaches, the data center distributed environment participates in deciding to achieve the performance metrics. The status of the failure rate is measured by the virtual machines running at hosts [9]. The reliability of the virtual machine is ascertained by the consideration of the end-to-end delay parameter. The authors only focused on workflow-based services in a heterogeneous environment. Attiya et al. expanded the simulated annealing algorithm for cloudlets allocation to a computing node. The objective and novelty of the work are the trust level of the methodology enhancement, and its efficiency is calculated in contrast with a branch and bound method [10].

The authors presented various multi-objective algorithms that depend on several performance evaluation metrics including reliability test, power utilization, make span, deadline constraint and on-demand resource scalability. The authors also described the tradeoff between two performance metrics, i.e., makespan and reliability of the presented system [11, 12]. Primarily the authors focused on optimization based on two performance metrics. Zhang et al. presented a genetic algorithm based on two performance metrics, reliability and power consumption. Nature-inspired population-based technique is tested in a non-homogeneous environment. The schedules are generated randomly in a non-homogeneous environment

[13]. The limitation of the proposed model is that the solution may be converse at the local optimal point. Fard et al. proposed a policy to minimize the Euclidean distance. Performance metrics included makespan, cost, power consumption and reliability optimization [14]. The results are validated using only a nature-inspired meta-heuristic technique. The performance metrics may be improved using the neural computing-based proposed model. The results may help in presenting a new proactive reliable scheduling technique.

Zhang et al. presented a novel technique for reliability improvement using power consumption constraints. The performance measurement parameters are estimated using infrastructure as a service delivery model [15]. The second category of fault-aware provisioning includes the reactive fault tolerance policy which manages the tasks, not paying attention to cloudlet execution when the chance of failure increases. The chance of failure or failure rate increases at the data center level. Our objective includes suppressing the failure rate and increasing resource utilization. Several reactive approaches are proposed in the literature for handling the fault at the time of cloudlets execution and virtual machine reliability evaluation. Zhou et al. elaborated on an algorithm for optimal checkpointing [16]. The developed technique efficiently selects checkpoints of storage and recovery server inside the data center. Zhou et al. developed a novel technique using a checkpoint. The authors covered two algorithms: first the data center topology which includes the node communication feature, and the second algorithm which includes the checkpoint image storage features. This systematic way of organizing the research helps in reducing the checkpoint overhead. The novelty is measured using the simulation process.

There is an opportunity to improve the performance of the reviewed proactive and reactive techniques using a hybrid type of model. The hybrid type of model includes the natural science-based research designs for better performance of the data center network support service delivery model at the infrastructure, platform and application levels.

7.3 OUTCOMES OF THE RELATED WORKS

The outcomes of the related work exhibit that researchers are focused on the fault-aware, checkpoint-based, cost- and power-aware provisioning techniques. The state-of-the-art methodologies work in overloaded, underloaded and average conditions. The scheduling time of the tasks on virtual machines is high. The meta-heuristic techniques provide the local optimal solution using fabricated and real datasets. The proposed fault-aware power-efficient bat-ANN model improves the performance of the state-of-the-art methods. The performance is evaluated using multiple schedules which provide the training datasets.

7.4 PROPOSED MODEL

In the review section, we found that there are various challenging issues in fault-aware and power-efficient scheduling approaches. Our primary objective is to propose a reliable fault- and power-aware model which will consider multivariate objective parameters. The multi-variant parameters estimate the performance of the presented model and validate the results of the multilayer's perceptron model using state-of-the-art methods. The multilayer perceptron model accuracy improves using multiple schedules for the training of the proposed bat-ANN model. In this article we introduced a bat and feedforward deep neural network-based hybrid tasks scheduling technique. In state-of-the-art methods, researchers presented the scheduling mechanism based on static, dynamic and meta-heuristic techniques. The state-of-the-art methods, genetic and particle swarm optimization techniques, provide the local optimal solution using various performance evaluation parameters. There is an opportunity to improve the performance of the nature-inspired techniques. The performance metrics include specifically power and faults. The power- and fault-aware scheduling is introduced which focuses on power consumption, faults and efficiency using the total execution time of the tasks submitted to the virtual machines. The reliability of the power- and fault-aware scheduling is improved using the neural computing model. The hybrid bat-ANN technique is validated using a GA-ANN-based task scheduling technique. Our objective is to improve the performance of the power-efficient GA-ANN technique which outperforms the BB–BC-cost and simple genetic cost-aware and time-aware scheduling methodologies. This sub-section exhibits the details about multilayer perceptron model used for the quality of service improvement of the fault-aware scheduling technique.

7.4.1 Initialization

In the initialization phase the output layer, input layer and hidden layers for features classifications and the number of perceptrons in each layer are defined. The associated parameters, learning rate, population size, mutation rate, number of evolutions and activation function used in the hidden layers and output layers, are defined also. The efficiency of the multilayer-based proposed model is defined using these initialized parameters.

7.4.2 Training Datasets Preparations

In this phase a training dataset is prepared using the bat optimization approach using a fitness function to enhance the performance metrics of total execution time, fault rate and power consumption. This phase takes a heterogeneous combination of a variety of tasks along with a list of virtual machines available as resources. The input is given to the bat algorithm.

$$F(x) = \alpha * \text{Utilization} + \beta * \text{Total\_Execution\_time} \tag{7.1}$$

Where $\alpha + \beta = 1$.

$$\text{Total\_Execution\_time} = \sum_{\text{task\_}i=1}^{n} \frac{\text{Task\_Length}_i}{\text{MIPS}_j} \tag{7.2}$$

The output of the training datasets preparation phase is a predicted schedule with the least execution time and power consumption and low fault rate. The outcome is a combination of tasks ID and the virtual machine ID allocated to VM. The list is divided into two parts of 80% and 20%, where the first part is given for multilayer neural network model training and 20% is given for testing the trained multilayer perceptron model and error correction using backpropagation.

7.4.3 Multilayer Perceptron Model Design

In this phase a multilayer perceptron model is designed using the parameters of the initialization phase. The model consists of an input layer, output layer and multiple hidden layers respectively. The Leaky Relue and sigmoid activation functions are used in the hidden layers and output layers respectively. Figure 7.1 also exhibits the multilayer artificial neural network. The multilayer feedforward neural network consists of multiple nodes in each layer. The nodes in each layer are divided into pre-activation (aggregation) and activation (nonlinearity) parts. The output of an adaptive multilayer perceptron model presents the reliable virtual machine identity which handles the user requests or cloudlets with low failure probability. It uses a feedforward neural computing model for achieving the target values of the reliable virtual machine. The performance of the ANN with bio-inspired techniques is measured using the state-of-the-art approaches for reliable scheduling. The artificial neural network is trained using different learning

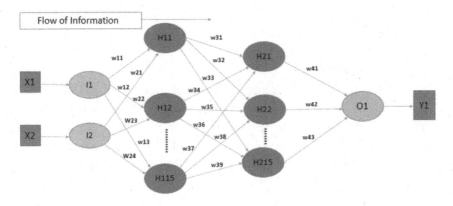

FIGURE 7.1 The architecture of the feedforward neural network for fault-aware scheduling in cloud.

rates. The accuracy of the output depends on the parameters used for training. The perceptron model performance depends on the training mechanism, the number of layers (hidden) and nodes and the activation parameters used at the perceptron level.

The state-of-the-art methods covered all the static, dynamic and bio-inspired meta-heuristic techniques for the fault, taking into account efficient resource allocation on reliable virtual machines. There is an opportunity for the improvement of the quality of service. Optimization criteria improve further using the meta-heuristic technique with the human brain computation process or artificial neural network. The artificial neural network with a meta-heuristic approach provides better results than standalone nature-inspired meta-heuristic techniques. Perceptrons and their connection strengths (edge weight) and bias values adjust for input datasets. The schedule sequences generate for the different evolution or iteration of the meta-heuristic technique. The trained neural network is used for the prediction of the appropriate virtual machine identity which executes the tasks without any fault. The output layer generates legitimate output after the learning or training process. Better results are achieved using the ANN model with bio-inspired meta-heuristic approaches. The strength of connection among the perceptron, and model trains using datasets in a cloud environment. Researchers have tried to solve the problem of fault-aware job scheduling in cloud computing. The inspired trained model helps in the optimal distribution of cloud resources. The researchers solve the issue of fault-aware job scheduling in scalable cloud aura using static, dynamic, bio-inspired meta-heuristic approaches. Our objective is to improve the performance of task scheduling based on the neural network model trained using the bat optimization technique.

7.4.4 Model Training

In this phase, the designed multilayer perceptron model is trained with 80% of the training data prepared to design a trained model. This phase is responsible for setting the weights of the neural network which defines the accuracy and efficiency level of the multilayer neural network. The training process of the model initializes the weight and bias parameters. The process repeats until the target values are grasped. The target values of the proposed model include the virtual machine identity, which takes minimum completion time of the tasks. The training process predicts an appropriate value of the unknown variables. The training mechanism includes the error correction-based mechanism and memory-based mechanism. The optimal trained multilayer neural network provides the optimal global solution with accuracy and stability. The available data should be categorized by applying a rule of thumb, i.e., 80% of available dataset is used for training, and the remaining 20% of data is used to test the output. The activation function of the nodes in hidden layers is measured using the Leaky Relue activation function.

$$\text{Leaky Relue Activation function} = \tag{7.3}$$
$$f(x) = \{ .01^* x \text{ if } x < 0, \ x \text{ if } x \geq 0 \}$$

The quality of service is measured using the optimization criteria power consumption and fault rate for resource utilization. The input layer forwards the weight to the hidden layers, and the hidden layers use the activation function and forward the results of the perceptron to the output layer. The activation function of a host defines the output of the host which is given as a set of inputs. This prominent feature of the activation function plays its role in computational artificial neural networks. Equation 7.3 exhibits the probabilistic activation function which includes the Leaky Relue function for the calculation of the perceptron values. The proposed ANN-based power- and fault-aware resource provisioning technique includes two inputs, one output and multiple hidden layers. The model is trained for the dataset or workload size, one-tenth of the user-defined workload. Two matrices are used for training input and training output. The training input size = 100×2, and the training output size is 100×1.

The workload size for the training dataset includes 100 tasks, which are 10% of the user-defined workload.

7.4.5 Error Backpropagation and Correction

Here our objective is to obtain the desired output. The desired output is obtained only after a proper neural network is designed. The feedforward method of the computation process is used in the forward direction. The computation in each of the neurons in the hidden and output layers is performed using the activation function. Figure 7.1 exhibits the computation function (activation function). The neurons of the adjacent layers are connected using connection weights and biases.

The proposed model follows the error correction learning mechanism. The error correction learning mechanism improves the quality of service using a cost function (δ_k). The goal is to minimize the cost function using the signal flow graph of the ANN model as shown in Figure 7.1. The error correction learning mechanism measures the error using Equation 7.4.

$$e_k(n) = d_k(n) - y_k(n) \tag{7.4}$$

$$\delta_k = \frac{1}{2} * e_k^2(n) \tag{7.5}$$

In Equation 7.4 and Equation 7.5, the parameter $d_k(n)$ denotes the expected output, $y_k(n)$ shows the exact output and $e_k(n)$ is the error, and δ_k is the cost function used in the learning process of the ANN model respectively.

7.4.6 Task Scheduling

In this phase, the neural network trained model is used to schedule the tasks in real time. The accuracy and efficiency of the multilayer perceptron model depend on the training process. The training process depends on the frequency tuning bat optimization technique which generates the training dataset. The tasks scheduling phase generates an optimal schedule using the performance metrics power and fault rate specifically.

7.4.7 Algorithm of the Proposed Resource Provisioning Technique Bat-ANN

7.4.7.1 Bat Optimization Approach

The state-of-the-art methods include meta-heuristic techniques which provide an optimal solution to the scheduling problem in a cloud environment. The performance of the nature-inspired technique can be improved using artificial intelligence approaches. In this article, we proposed a hybrid technique, i.e., Bat-ANN. The probability-based optimization technique is integrated with the artificial deep neural network. The proposed model follows the echolocation characteristics of microbats. The echolocation behavior of the bat is inherited in the proposed bat-ANN model. The bat-ANN hybrid technique improves the performance of the simple meta-heuristic optimization bat algorithm for the scheduling of tasks on cloud. The bat algorithm is also known as a frequency tuning algorithm which provides an optimal solution of the combinatorial optimization and scheduling. Each bat is assigned a random frequency in a search space. The parameters associated with the bat algorithm are obtained using Equations 7.6, 7.7 and 7.8 respectively.

$$f_i = f_{\min} + (f_{\max} - f_{\min}) * \beta \tag{7.6}$$

Where $\beta \varepsilon [0,1]$, and min f_i denotes the frequency of the ith bat,

$$v_i^t = v_i^{t-1} + (x_i^{t-1} - x_*) * f_i \tag{7.7}$$

Where v_i^t denotes the velocity of the ith bat in the tth iteration.

$$x_i = x_i^{t-1} + v_i^t \tag{7.8}$$

Where x_i denotes the position of the ith bat in a search space. The bat technique helps to train the neural network. The hybrid approach gives better results than simple bio-inspired, nature-inspired and frequency tuning techniques. The bat algorithm initializes the frequency, position and velocity of all the bats. The pulse frequency $f_i x_i$ is defined. The pulse rate emission r_i and loudness parameter A_i are also initialized. In a simple bat algorithm the following steps are used:

1. Initialize the bat population, its position, velocity, frequency.

2. Initialize echolocation parameters of all bats.

3. Initialize pulse frequency f_i at x_i.

4. Initialize pulse rate r_i and loudness A_i.

While (termination condition).

Generate new solutions by adjusting the frequency and updating the velocities and locations.

End while.

7.4.8 Proposed Bat-ANN Task Scheduling Algorithm

The proposed model is divided into the following steps:

1. Initialize.

2. Prepare training datasets using a probability-based bat optimization technique.

3. Design a deep neural network and train the model using training datasets generated in step 2.

4. Perform tasks scheduling on a virtual machine using the trained model.

5. Generate an optimal schedule.

6. Repeat steps 2–4 until the convergence condition is satisfied.

Figure 7.2 presents the flow diagram of the proposed bat-ANN model. The flow diagram exhibits the pictorial representation of the proposed algorithm bat-ANN. It shows a clear picture of the role of the bat optimization technique and optimization of the edge weight with the multilayer perceptron model. Hence the training dataset is generated using a bat algorithm. Input datasets of virtual machine ID and cloudlet ID are provided using the nature-inspired frequency tuning evolutionary technique.

7.5 RESULTS AND DISCUSSIONS

Simulation is performed using Cloudsim 3.0. The simulation uses workload traces for real-time task simulation which is an SWF format workload file from parallel workload, a free open-source dataset from parallel workload repository (Table 7.1).

The performance evaluation of the bat-ANN model is performed using the following performance metrics:

1. Total execution time/makespan (millisecond).

2. Average start time (millisecond).

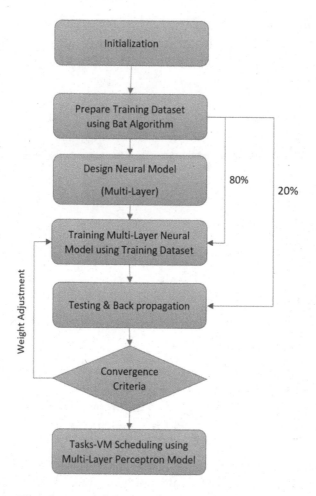

FIGURE 7.2   Flow diagram of the proposed bat-ANN scheduling technique in cloud.

3. Average finish time (millisecond).

4. Number of completed tasks.

5. Number of failed tasks.

Figure 7.3(a), (b) showcases a comparison of the average start times for a set of tasks using the proposed algorithm and existing approaches using five virtual machines and ten virtual machines as resources. The result shows the proposed algorithm performs better than existing algorithms. The study assesses the performance of start time with increasing load and scaling resources.

TABLE 7.1   Configuration Parameters of User Tasks

Task Parameters	Values
Task length	200–40000
Input size	300 byte
Output size	300 byte
PE	1/2

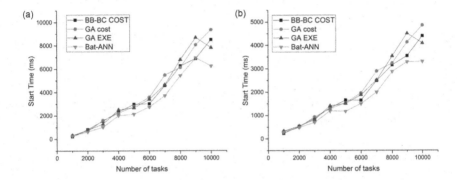

FIGURE 7.3   (a) Comparison start time vs number of tasks for five VM. (b) Comparison start time vs number of tasks for ten VM.

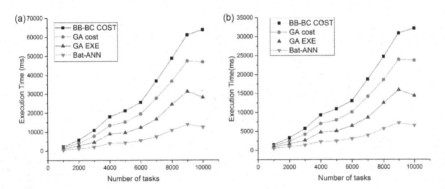

FIGURE 7.4   (a) Comparison execution time vs number of tasks for five VM. (b) Comparison execution time vs number of tasks for ten VM.

Figure 7.4(a), (b) showcases a comparison of execution times for a set of tasks using the proposed algorithm and existing approaches using five virtual machines and ten virtual machines as resources. The result shows the proposed algorithm performs better than existing algorithms. This experiment is performed to study the performance of the proposed algorithm in underloaded and overloaded conditions.

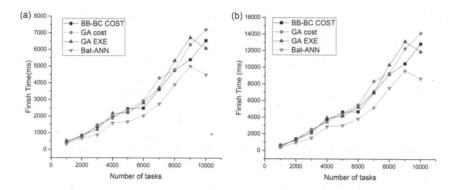

FIGURE 7.5   (a) Comparison finish time vs number of tasks for five VM. (b) Comparison finish time vs number of tasks for ten VM.

Figure 7.5(a), (b) showcases a comparison of finish times for a set of tasks using the proposed algorithm and existing approaches using five virtual machines and ten virtual machines as resources. The result shows the proposed algorithm performs better than existing algorithms. The study assesses the performance of finish time with increasing load and scaling resources.

Figure 7.6(a), (b) showcases a study of completed tasks for a set of tasks using the proposed algorithm and existing approaches using five virtual machines and ten virtual machines as resources and increasing load over the data center. The result shows the proposed algorithm performs better than existing algorithms. Similarly the experiment is performed to find the improvement in the number of tasks completed.

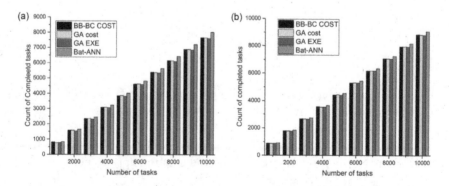

FIGURE 7.6   (a) Comparison of number of completed tasks vs number of tasks for five VM. (b) Comparison of number of completed tasks vs number of tasks for ten VM.

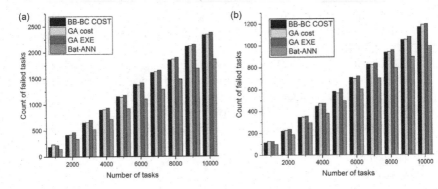

FIGURE 7.7 (a) Comparison of number of failed tasks vs number of tasks for five VM. (b) Comparison of number of failed tasks vs number of tasks for ten VM.

The experiment results are shown in Figure 7.7(a) and (b) which shows improvement in performance with increasing load and resources.

7.6 CONCLUSION AND FUTURE WORKS

In this paper, an efficient task scheduling scheme was presented for task scheduling in cloud infrastructure. The projected bat-ANN model outperforms the genetic approach and existing techniques. The results section shows that the projected model performs better than the existing techniques for cloud IaaS. Performance is computed using the performance metrics: Average finish time (ms), average start time (ms), total execution time, fault rate, number of tasks completed and number of tasks failed. This work is focused only on task scheduling in cloud using a bat algorithm. The work has proposed a fault-tolerant model with a high quality of service. In future work, the proposed model will be used for resource scheduling on host and migration approaches for the better utilization of resources to improve the running cost of cloud applications with optimal resources.

REFERENCES

1. Ghrera SP et al. Power and fault aware reliable resource allocation for cloud infrastructure. *Physics Procedia* [Internet]. 78(December 2015), 457–63 (2016).

2. Kathpal C. & Garg R. Survey on fault-tolerance-aware scheduling in cloud computing. *Information and Communication Technology for Competitive Strategies*, 275–283. (2019).

3. T.J. Charity & G.C. Hua. Resource reliability using fault tolerance in cloud computing. In: 2016 2nd International Conference on Next Generation Computing Technologies (NGCT), pp. 65–71. IEEE (2016).

4. Li, K., Mei, J. et al. Fault-tolerant dynamic rescheduling for heterogeneous computing systems. *J. Grid Comput.* Dec 1;13(4), 507–25 (2015).

5. Rehani, N. & Garg, R. Meta-heuristic based reliable and green workflow scheduling in cloudcomputing. *Int. J. Syst. Assur. Eng. Manag.* 9(4), 1–10.

6. Qin, X. & Jiang, H.. A dynamic and reliability-driven scheduling algorithm for parallel real-time jobs executing on heterogeneous clusters. *J. Parallel Distrib. Comput.* 65(8), 885–900 (2005).

7. Zhou, A., Wang, S., Cheng, B., Zheng, Z., Yang, F., Chang, R.N., Lyu, M.R. & Buyya, R. Cloud service reliability enhancement via virtual machine placement optimization. *IEEE Trans. Serv. Comput.* 10(6), 902–913 (2016).

8. Garg, R. & Rehani, N. Reliability-aware workflow scheduling using monte carlo failure estimation in cloud. In: Proceedings of International Conference on Communication and Networks, pp. 139–153. Springer, Singapore (2017).

9. Zhu, M.M & Cao, F. Distributed workflow mapping algorithm for maximized reliability under end-to-end delay constraint. *J. Supercomput.* 66(3), 1462–1488 (2013).

10. Hamam, Y. & Attiya, G. Task allocation for maximizing reliability of distributed systems: a simulated annealing approach. *J. Parallel Distrib. Comput.* 66(10), 1259–1266 (2006).

11. Dongarra, J.J., Jeannot, E., et al. Bi-objective scheduling algorithms for optimizing makespan and reliability on heterogeneous systems. In: Proceedings of the Nineteenth Annual ACM Symposium on Parallel Algorithms and Architectures, pp. 280–288. ACM (2007).

12. Wang, X., Yeo, C.S., Buyya, R., Su, J. Optimizing the makespan and reliability for workflow applications with reputation and a look-ahead genetic algorithm. *Fut. Generat. Comput. Syst.* 27(8), 1124–1134 (2011).

13. Zhang, L., Li, K., et al. Bi-objective workflow scheduling of the energy consumption and reliability in heterogeneous computing systems. *Inf. Sci.* 379, 241–256 (2017).

14. Fard, H.M., Prodan, R., Barrionuevo, et al. A multi-objective approach for workflow scheduling in heterogeneous environments. In: Proceedings of the 2012 12th IEEE/ ACM International Symposium on Cluster, Cloud and Grid Computing (CCGRID 2012), pp. 300–309. IEEE Computer Society (2012).

15. Zhang, L., Li, K., Xu, Y., et al. Maximizing reliability with energy conservation for parallel task scheduling in a heterogeneous cluster. *Inf. Sci.* 319, 113–131 (2015).
16. Li, J., Zhou, A., & Sun, Q., Enhancing reliability via checkpointing in cloud computing systems. *China Commun.* 14(7), 1–10 (2017).

CHAPTER 8

Energy-Efficient VM Placement Using Backpropagation Neural Network and Genetic Algorithm

Oshin Sharma, Hemraj Saini
and Geetanjali Rathee

CONTENTS

DOI: 10.1201/9781003185376-8

8.1 INTRODUCTION

The proliferation of cloud computing can support numerous services such as servers, networks, storage and applications for e-sciences as well as e-business and many others. This architecture of cloud computing is a huge pool of virtualized resources which are readily usable and easily accessible such as platform, hardware and services (e.g., memory, .Net, CPU, Java, email and HR, etc.). These pools of resources are provisioned on a pay per usage model, where the availability and guarantee of resources are offered by cloud service providers by the means of service level agreements (SLA) [1]. The deployment of data centers requires large amounts of energy to run multiple servers and for the cooling of the electronic devices used inside data centers. From the data center knowledge report [2], it has been found that 55% of the energy consumption of data centers is due to data equipment and servers and 30% is due to cooling equipment. These data centers are very expensive to maintain, and moreover, they also have adverse effects on the environment.

Virtualization is the most applicable topic which provides better QoS while dealing with server/VM consolidation, autoscaling, energy conservation, load balancing, etc. [3–8]. Virtualization runs multiple operating systems on a single machine while dealing with the problem of resource utilization and energy inefficiency. Various tools are widely used in data centers to make use of the virtualization technique such as VMware, KVM, XEN and many more [9, 10]. The inappropriate allocation of VMs degrades the performance and quality of services. The migration of virtual machines and their mapping over the right physical machine can diminish the energy consumption of data centers and deliver good QoS which may further reduce the SLA violation [11]. Appropriate mapping of a virtual machine over a physical machine reduces the amount of hardware in use and improves resource utilization and power and energy efficiency [12]. Figure 8.1 displays the scenario of VM placement using a virtualization technique where we have assessed eight physical machines (PMs). These physical machines vary from 15% to 50% utilization. Thus, the main aim of an optimal VM placement process is to map the virtual machines over physical machines in such a way that fewer PMs should be used by improving their utilization rates and switching the rest of the PMs into hibernate mode or switching them off.

The workload in the cloud environment is dynamic in nature; therefore, many different heuristics have been proposed by researchers considering the extensions of greedy approaches such as first fit, best fit,

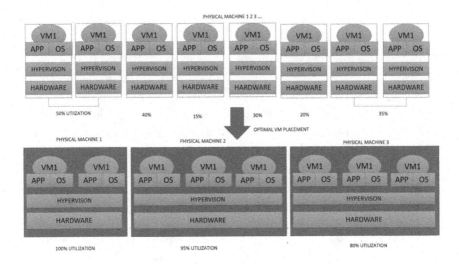

FIGURE 8.1 Example of an optimal VM placement.

first fit decreasing and best fit decreasing to solve this problem such as power-aware best fit decreasing (PABFD) [13], modified best fit decreasing (MBFD) [14], TPOSIS [15], EPOBFD [4] and many more. However, these greedy approaches do not guarantee the generation of optimal solutions as they easily fall into local optima and it became very hard to find the global optimal solution due to single point of search strategy. Therefore, the most powerful methods to deal with these problems are population-based evolutionary computing (EC) algorithms such as genetic algorithms (GA), ant colony optimization (ACO), particle swarm optimization (PSO) and many others.

This article contributes as follows:

- A meta-heuristic approach to VM placement to achieve energy efficiency.

- The proposed BPGA uses bio-inspired optimization during the VM consolidation process.

- The proposed BPGA model has been tested in the CloudSim [16] which shows that it is scalable for heterogeneous data centers.

- This research provides a generalized comparison of classical bin packing techniques with new meta heuristics techniques such as genetic algorithms, ant colony optimization and multi-objective optimization.

The remaining layout of the manuscript is described as follows: Section 8.2 presents the most related work for the VM placement or VM consolidation process using different techniques and Section 8.3 gives a description of the system model that we have used in our work. The problem description of multi-objective optimization for VM placement and the framework of data centers is discussed in Section 8.4. A detailed description of the proposed BPGA model for VM placement is given in Section 8.5, while Section 8.6 provides the experimental set up for simulations of VM placement using the CloudSim simulator along with analytical and statistical results for the comparison of results with other existing reference VM placement algorithms, and Section 8.7 lays out the conclusion of the current work with some future directions.

8.2 TRADITIONAL VM PLACEMENT WORK

In this section, we will discuss the prior and most relevant work related to VM migration and placement that aims to address the issues related to energy consumption, SLA violation and other performance parameters inside data centers. A lot of research has been conducted in this area of cloud computing where these issues have been handled without or with VM migration and has been considered as the best technique. But the process of VM migration inside data centers is not straightforward for energy management, as it involves the overall VM consolidation process for the implementation. Moreover, the VM consolidation process has four different steps [14]. All these steps can efficiently manage the energy issues of data centers. The authors have investigated different heuristics as well as meta-heuristics techniques to handle these issues. First architecture for the energy management of virtualized data centers has been developed by Nathuji et al. [17] by using the concept of live migration of virtual machines to consolidate them on a single server. The process of VM consolidation by making use of the dynamic migration of VMs on fewer hosts also has been presented by Lim et al. [18] for energy management inside a virtualized environment. Later, Goiri et al. [19] proposed a profit-oriented multi-objective algorithm for VM placement that considered the performance of data centers after migration in terms of energy efficiency, SLA violations and virtualization overhead. Similarly, Verma et al. [20, 21] and Ghribi et al. [22] proposed VM placement and VM allocation algorithms for minimizing the number of hosts used and to minimize the consumption of energy by considering the performance of data centers as well as migration cost inside data centers.

Beloglazov et al. [14, 23, 24] proposed energy-aware heuristics using the concept of VM migration for the dynamic allocation of VMs according to current resource utilization [25–29]. A new technique of consolidation has been advocated by Bila et al. [30] which migrates the idle virtual machines to reduce the consumption of energy. The work presented by Zohu et al. [31] is for the improvement of the reliability of cloud services by using network and storage resources; their algorithm used the characteristics of the network architecture of data centers to minimize the resource usage of the network, but instead of using these resources our work focuses on improving the usage of memory and CPU resources. For this, the virtual machine will be placed on that node which will be selected by our BPGA model while maintaining both the energy efficiency and performance of the data center. To achieve an optimal placement or migration of virtual machines, the consideration of current resources such as utilization of memory and processors is very important. These resources are the main power-consuming units observed from papers [14, 32]. The proposed BPGA model also efficiently deals with the energy optimization at both the memory and processor level. Along with this, it also improves the resource utilization by minimizing the number of hosts used and number of VM migrations. VM placement helps in lowering the energy consumption of idle or free resources by keeping them aside and switching them off or into sleep mode. The focus on conserving the free or idle resources is to improve the energy efficiency and to lower the SLA violation defined in [33]. In the most recent survey on VM consolidation [34], Khichar G. S. et al. also proposed an algorithm MC_MC using the knapsack technique to reduce the migrations and energy consumption, whereas in [35] Bajoria V. et al. proposed a different policy for the minimization of energy consumption which considers both the cost and time efficiency of an algorithm. Cost efficiency would be provided while prioritizing the CPU utilization, whereas time efficiency would be provided by prioritizing the degradation of performance. Li Z. et al. [36] provided VM placement using anti-collocation constraints where they have proposed a page rank-based algorithm to find the best VM-PM map for full utilization of the host with the minimum amount of energy consumption. Maiyza A. I. et al. [37] proposed the MMTMC2 algorithm for VM migration to improve the overall VM consolidation process. Their idea was to maintain the number of live migrations and network load in cloud data centers.

With the increase in the complexity of distributed services provided by the cloud environment, it is essential to propose some techniques that are more sustainable and scalable for heterogeneous environments. Additionally, they can deal with the energy crisis that is growing day by day.

Current research work focuses on bio-inspired computing and meta heuristic techniques to handle these issues because they have ability to adjust the search space automatically, although they have a large search space.

The proposed study focuses on the optimal balance between energy consumption and QoS. Accordingly, we present the BPGA method with the following major differences as compared to previous works: First, the presented VM consolidation model focuses on the balance between energy consumption and the host's workload stability during ongoing consolidation. Second, using NSGA multi-objective optimization or a set of Pareto-optimal solutions along with backpropagation the neural network is itself an innovation as compared to previous literature. Next, searching the final optimum results in the solution space (e.g., population) is performed by BPGA, and it not only guarantees the global optimization result but accelerates the evolutionary process. At last, VM consolidation using two different passes together guarantees the reliability of the results. Extensive experiments have been conducted on two different datasets which demonstrates that improved BPGA reduces the energy consumption without degrading the QoS. Unlike our previous work, here we used Planet Lab datasets and Bitbrains [38] datasets for the validation of the BPGA model.

8.3 SYSTEM MODEL

The system model consists of heterogeneous resources such as CPU utilization defined in millions of instructions per second, network bandwidth, disk capacity and RAM within data centers. The data center framework used in our experiments is shown in Figure 8.2, and similarly the energy and power model is explained in detail in Section 8.3.2.

8.3.1 Data Center Framework

The framework for VM placement optimization in our work is shown in Figure 8.2 in which we have two main components for energy-efficient VM allocation on physical machines: (1) VM placement analyzer and (2) SLA manager. The VM analyzer checks the resource availability on servers for the allocation of VMs, and the SLA manager checks the level of violation after every placement and notifies the analyzer.

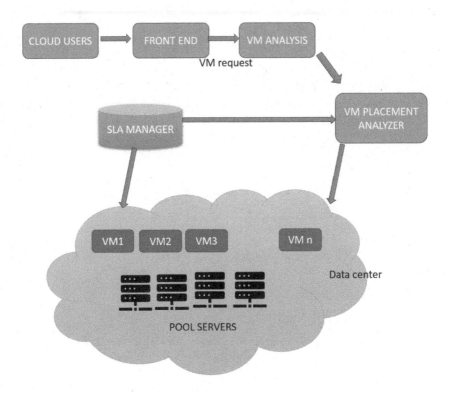

FIGURE 8.2   Framework for virtualized data center.

8.3.2 Energy Consumption Modeling

Different components like memory occupied, disk storage, network interface and the CPU are responsible for energy consumption. In [39], it has been shown that the power consumption and CPU utilization of servers have a linear relationship between them.

The CPU utilization of a server may change with time due to variable workload and thus, the CPU utilization is represented as a function of time $U(t)$. Therefore, the total energy consumption (EC) of a physical server can be calculated as the integral of the power consumption over a period [14]. In Equation 8.1 and Equation 8.2 PCbusy represents the power consumption when the machine is fully utilized and PCidle represents the value of power consumption when the machine is idle or 0% utilized. For our simulations Table 8.1 shows the power consumption of the server when it is idle and fully utilized. The power consumption of these servers is taken from SPEC power benchmark [40].

TABLE 8.1   Power Consumption of Servers (kWh) [60]

.Server	Idle	10%	20%	30%	40%	50%	60%	70%	80%	90%	100%
HPProLiant G4	86	89.4	92.6	96	99.5	102	106	108	112	114	117
HPProLiant G5	93.7	97	101	105	110	116	121	125	129	133	135
IBMServerX3250	41.6	46.7	52.3	57.9	65.4	73	80.7	89.5	99.6	105	113
IBM Server x3550	58.4	98	109	118	128	140	153	170	189	205	222
Acer AT150 F1	65.4	113	125	136	150	165	183	199	215	229	244
Acer AR320 F1	39.6	47.3	55	63.4	71.9	80.3	89.8	97.9	107	116	124

$$EC = \int_{t0}^{t1} P(U(t)) dt \tag{8.1}$$

$$PC = \begin{cases} (PCbusy_i - PCidle_i) \times U_i^{PC} + PC_i^{idle}, & U_i > 0 \\ 0, & \text{othewise} \end{cases} \tag{8.2}$$

8.4 PROBLEM FORMULATION AND SOLUTION

In this section, we discuss the formulation of VM placement and its solution using multi-objective optimization. NSGA has been used for the optimal mapping of VMs.

8.4.1 Multi-Objective VM Placement Problem

A population-based approach is the key feature of multi-objective optimization. Along with this, we have used the concept of Pareto-dominance in the selection of VMs.

The problem of multi-objective optimization can be solved with a set of n number of objectives. These objectives need to be maximized or minimized depending upon the problem (minimization in our case).

$$\text{minimize} f(X) = \{f(X1, X2, \ldots\ldots Xn)\} \tag{8.3}$$

Equation 8.3 represents the problem of minimization where X represents the decision variables. The solutions of multi-objective optimization do not provide the optimal solution for all the objectives. Pareto-optimal solutions are most suitable in these situations which provide trade-off results. These trade-off solutions have a set of non- dominated solutions which further provide best solutions for several objectives [41].

A solution S from solution space 'sp' is said to be Pareto-optimal, if there is no other solution P that exists which dominates solution S. Moreover, solution S dominates solution P or S has a better non-dominated rank than P, i.e., $R_S < R_P$ (rank of S and P), if both of the following equations are true:

Condition 1: If solution S is as good as solution P for all the objectives:

$$\forall j \in [1,2....n] f_j(S) \leq f_j(P) \qquad (8.4)$$

Condition 2: If solution S is severely better than P for at least one objective:

$$\exists j \in [1,2....n] f_j(S) < f_j(P) \qquad (8.5)$$

All the solutions which are not dominated by any other solutions are called non-dominated solutions, and they together constitute a front in the solution space known as the non-dominated front; also the set of solutions in the non-dominated fronts are known as Pareto-optimal solutions. The most tedious step in this concept is to find the set of non-dominated solutions. In our work, to find the set of non-dominated solutions the following steps are used [58] with Z number of solutions, and each has N number of objectives:

Step 1: Start with $i = 1$.

Step 2: Compare solution S_i and P_i for their domination rank using the above mentioned conditions for all N objectives.

Step 3: If S_i is dominated by P_i, then mark S_i as dominated and go to step 2 by incrementing $i = i++$.

Step 4: If all the solutions ($i = 1$ to Z) are considered, go to the next step; otherwise go to step 2 by incrementing i.

Step 5: Solutions which are not marked as dominated are non-dominated solutions.

8.4.2 VM Placement Optimization

Here the VM placement has been optimized as the number of V virtual machines need to be mapped on number of M physical machines. It has been assumed that C_i amount of CPU utilization is requested from each VM and Th_{uj} is the threshold for CPU utilization, Mem_i is the amount of memory requested by each VM and *Thm*$_j$ is the threshold for memory utilization. We have also considered two variables L_{ij} and Q_j for the investigation of the assignment of VMs. Using these assumptions, we have minimized some objectives such as migration count, SLA violations and cost of the data center. Thus, the problem of VM placement can be formalized as:

Energy Consumption:

$$\sum_{j=1}^{M} EC_j = \sum_{j=1}^{M} \left[X_j \times \left(PCbusy_j - PCidle_j \right) \times \sum_{i=1}^{V} L_{ij} \cdot C_i + PCidle_j \right] \quad (8.6)$$

SLA Violation:

$$\sum_{j=1}^{M} SLAV = \left[\frac{1}{M} \sum_{j=1}^{M} \frac{T_{si}}{T_{ai}} \right] * \left[\frac{1}{V} \sum_{i=1}^{V} \frac{C_{dj}}{C_{rj}} \right] \quad (8.7)$$

Number of Host Used:

$$\sum_{j=1}^{M} y_j \text{ where } \begin{cases} y_j = 1 & \text{if } \sum_{i=1}^{V} Q_{ji} \geq 1 \\ y_j = 0 & \text{otherwise} \end{cases} \quad (8.8)$$

Migration Count:

$$\frac{1 - \dfrac{MC_j}{\Sigma MC}}{P - \displaystyle\sum_{j=1}^{M} \dfrac{MC_j}{\Sigma MC}} \quad (8.9)$$

Cost Function:

$$CT = \sum_{t=to}^{T} \left(CTP \sum_{j=0}^{M} HA_{tj} + CTV \sum_{j=1}^{M} SV_{tj} \right) \quad (8.10)$$

In Equation 8.7, SLA violation has been calculated as: T_{si} is the total time for which the host experienced 100% utilization, T_{ai} represents the time for which the host remains active, C_{dj} is the estimate of performance degradation caused by migration and C_{rj} is the total CPU capacity of the virtual machine. For minimizing the number of hosts in Equation 8.8, we have taken a decision variable X_{ji}, which shows whether host j ($y_j = 1$) is used or not ($y_j = 0$). The cost function has been calculated as *CTPtp* and *CTVtp* where *CTP* is the cost of power and *tp* is time period (energy per unit time) and *CTV* is the cost of SLA violation per unit time.

8.5 PROPOSED ENERGY-EFFICIENT BPGA OPTIMIZATION MODEL

In [42, 43] we have discussed the first three steps of VM consolidation, and here we have proposed a BPGA VM placement method for energy minimization and the improvement of resource utilization. It directly contributes towards green computing by the minimization of energy consumption after reducing the active machines.

The current work presents an energy-aware virtual machine placement (VMP) technique for cloud data centers which is based on the genetic algorithm (NSGA) and the biological neural network (BPNN) and named the BPGA model shown in Figure 8.3. This technique tries to place the virtual machines that we have selected from our previous work [43] to another active host so that their mapping minimizes the energy consumption by reducing the number of active hosts inside the data center. This BPGA model works in two passes. Details of these two passes have been discussed as follows:

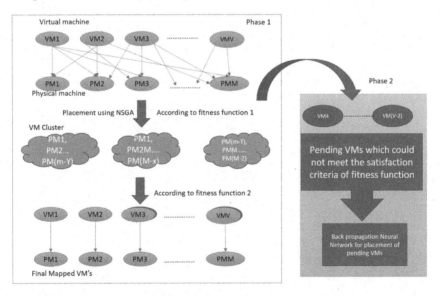

FIGURE 8.3　BPGA model for VM placement.

8.5.1 Pass 1: Non-Dominated Sorting Genetic Algorithm (NSGA)

Step 1. Initially, we can map any VM over any machine, but satisfying constraint 11 is very important which says that every VM needs to be mapped on one single machine.

$$\sum_{j=1}^{M} X_{ji} = 1 \forall j \in PM \wedge \forall i \in VM \tag{8.11}$$

Step 2. The total amount of resources requested by virtual machines will be calculated along with the capacity of the physical machine that provides the resources, and it will be checked if they satisfy the fitness function 1. If yes, then the value of fitness function 1 will be calculated and VM clusters will be created in which VMs will be arranged according to their ranks [44]. By VM clusters, we mean that PMs within these clusters are the options for the mapping of VMs. Moreover, if these constraints are not satisfied by the VMs than those pending VMs will be forwarded to pass 2 without checking the objective function 2.

Fitness Function 1: Resource Capacity

CPU (*C*) and memory utilization (*Mem*) are the two main resources that we have considered in our work. In the chromosome representation of the genetic algorithm each value of gene array represents the placement destination of a virtual machine. For the *j*th physical machine, suppose that it can carry *m* virtual machines, then the resource dimension array for VM *m* carried on *j*th physical machine can be expressed as: $[C_{j1}, C_{j2}, \dots, C_{jm}]$ and $[Mem_{j1}, Mem_{j2}, \dots, Mem_{jm}]$. The total value of resource properties are:

$$RC_j = C_j + Mem_j \tag{8.12}$$

$$Fitness_{F1} = \frac{1}{RC_j} \tag{8.13}$$

Algorithm 1 Pass 1 of the BPGA model Using NSGA

```
1      Input: VM list, Host list
2      Output: VM-PM placement map
3      Allocated host = null, Cando_List = null,
       min_energy=MAX
4      Tournament size[][] = null \\ tournament size
       will be equal to VM count * host count
5      Objective1.NSGA= find_fit (Host capacity, VM
       requirements)
```

```
6       For each VM in VM List
7         For Hostcount = 1: Hostcount
8           If (Host_fufill( VM requirements))
9           {
10      Cando_List[Hostcount][0] = host_id
11      Cando_List[Hostcount][1] = VM-id
12          }
13        Else
14        {
15      BPNN( )
16        }
17        End for
18      End for each
19      Objective 2.NSGA = selectionbestfit(
        Cando_List[])
20      If host.containing.VM >1 \\ if VM has more than
        one PMs available for mapping
21      For each host in Cando_List[ ]
22        If (host. Energy <min_energy)
22          {
23            Allocated hosts = host
24      Min_energy = Energy
25          }
26      Return VM-PM Placement map (Allocated hosts)
```

Step 3. If objective function 1 is satisfied, then from the above generated VM clusters every virtual machine has more than one physical machine available for the mapping. Therefore, this step provides the final mapping of virtual machines over physical machines by calculating the value of fitness function 2, and physical machines which could be the destinations for the VMs will be arranged according to the ranking of their fitness value within the clusters, and according to that value, the physical machine will be chosen from every VM cluster for the placement of virtual machines. The value of energy consumption has been calculated in fitness function 2 (Figure 8.4).

Fitness Function 2: Energy Consumption

$$\text{Fitness}_{F2} = \frac{1}{\sum_{j=1}^{M} \left[ENCtotal \right]} \tag{8.14}$$

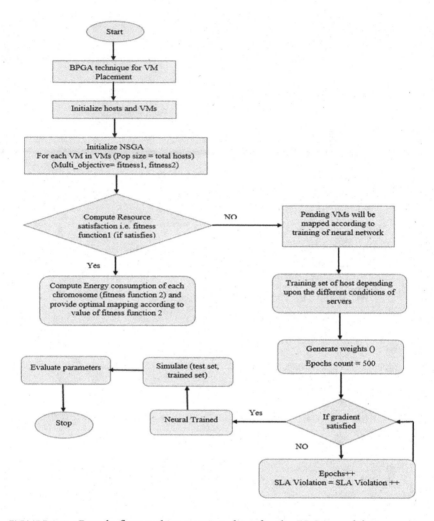

FIGURE 8.4 Pseudo flow and interaction chart for the BPGA model.

Algorithm 2: Pass 2 of the BPGA Model Using BPNN

```
1        Input : VM List, Host List
2        Output: VM-PM Placement map
3        TrainSet[][]
4        For each host in Host List
5         For (i = 1 to 11)  \\value of power consumption
          of servers on 11 different condition from idle
          to 100% utilized
6         Train_Set[host][i] = host[condition(i)]
7          End for
8        End for each
```

```
9       Total Epochs= 500 \\ total number of possible
        iterations
10      Initialize gradient_satisfied = 0
11      Term_weight[ ][ ]
12      While ( gradient not satisfied)
13        For each data in Train_Set([ ][ ])
14      Term_Weight[i, f] = a*data +b  \\ a and b are
        arbitrary values
15        End for
16      End While
17      MT = Mean(Term_Weight)
18      If (MT < gradient)
19        {
20      Term_weight = Term_weight + s
21        }
22      Else
23        {
24      Gradient_satisfied = 1
25        }
26      If (gradient_satisfied = 1) \\ neural training
        is complete
27        {
28      Test_Set[VM][i] = VM[conditions(i)] \\
        utilization of VM on 11 different conditions
        from idle to 100% utilized
29        }
30      For each VM in Test_Set
31      Allocated_Host = Simulate (Test_Set, Train_Set)
32      Assign VM to Allocated_Host
33      Return PM-VM Placement map (Allocated_ host)
```

Step 1: Initially the random variables are generated for the gradient. In the first iteration *gradient_satisfied* would be zero and turns out one if the gradient is satisfied. From Table 8.1, the utilization of servers from the value of 0 to 100% are used as the input weights for the *Term_weight*[][] matrix. Equation 8.15 shows the constraint for gradient satisfaction where *a* and *b* are random integer values.

$$\left(if\ gradient\_satisfied\ =\ =0\right)$$

$$Term\_Weight = generate\ Term\_Weight\left(data\right) \qquad (8.15)$$

$$= a*\left(data\right)+b\left(random\ integer\ values\ for\ a\ and\ b\right)$$

Step 2: In this step, the average value of weights and gradient will be checked in the hidden layer. If the random change in the average weight is less than the value of the gradient, then value of weight will be increased by the value of *s* calculated using Equation 8.16 for which first, we will find the mean value of *Term_Weight* known as *MT* and compare it with the gradient.

$$Term\_Weight = Term\_weight + s\big(Where\ s\ is\ random\ change\big)\big\{if\ MT < gradient\big\}$$
$$gradient\_satisfied = 1\big\{otherwise\big\}$$

$$(8.16)$$

Step 3: Now, the neural network is trained enough to work for a new set of inputs.

As with *Train_Set*, the matrix of *Test_Set* contains the energy consumption of VMs during the 11 different conditions of severs from idle to 100% utilized. The *Test_Set* matrix will be further passed to simulate function along with the *Train_Set* matrix for the allocation of the most appropriate host mentioned in Algorithm 3.

Algorithm 3: Simulate Function of Neural Network

```
1       Input: Test_Set, Train_Set
2       Output: Allocated_Host
3       Initialize Tts, Trs =0
4       Tts = Test_Set
5       Trs = Train_Set
6       [r] = size (Trs)
7       For (i = 1 to r)
8         MT = Mean(Trs)
9         MR = Mean(Tts)
10          If (MT < MR)
11          {
12      Allocated_Host = i
13          }
14      End for
```

8.6 PERFORMANCE EVALUATIONS

To evaluate the performance improvement made by the BPGA VM placement model, we have compared it with three existing reference algorithms: PABFD, GA and ACO. These reference algorithms are briefly described as follows:

TABLE 8.2 Configuration of Servers

Server	CPU Model	RAM (GB)	Frequency (MHz)	Cores
IBM Server x3250	Intel XeonX3480	8	2,933	4
IBM Server x3250	Intel Xeon X3470	16	3,067	12
Acer AT150 F1	Intel Xeon 5670	12	2,933	12
Acer AR320 F1	Intel Xeon 3470	8	2,933	4
HP ProLiant G4	Intel Xeon 3040	4	1,860	2
HP ProLiant G4	Intel Xeon 3075	8	2,933	2

TABLE 8.3 Instances of VMs [45]

VM Type	CPU (MIPS)	RAM (GB)
Extra large (high memory)	3,000	6
Medium (high CPU)	2,500	0.85
Extra large	2,000	3.75
Small	1,000	1.7
Micro	500	0.613

8.6.1 Experimental Setup

We have chosen the CloudSim simulation platform for our experimental setup, as it is very difficult to perform experiments in a real cloud environment. The data center environment consists of 800 servers with 6 different configurations. Table 8.2 provides the configuration of these servers and Table 8.3 shows five different instances of VMs that we have used here. Moreover, for the simulation environment we have considered real workload from ten days' data of the CoMoN Project [46].

8.6.2 Simulation Results and Comparison

In this section we have discussed the energy consumption, migration count and number of hosts used after placement by BPGA model. We have compared the results with GA, ACO and PABFD using PlanetLab datasets shown in Figures 8.5–8.8. Figure 8.5 depicts the lower number of hosts used by BPGA on the increase of VMs during every run.

Figure 8.6 shows the lower number of migrations taken by BPGA in comparison to PABFD, GA and ACO. BPGA finds the best suitable match for VM-PM with minimum energy consumption as we can see in Figure 8.7.

8.7 CONCLUSIONS AND FUTURE SCOPE

Green computing is a very popular area for research these days. The growing demand for computing resources, applications and storage in data

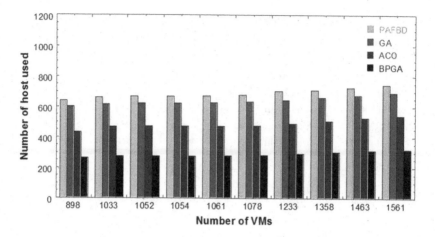

FIGURE 8.5   Number of hosts used vs number of VMs (PlanetLab Trace).

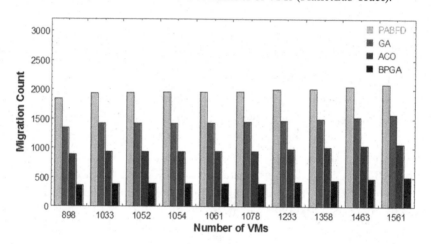

FIGURE 8.6   Migration count vs number of VMs (PlanetLab Trace).

centers is the main source of carbon emissions. Thus, effective energy management is very helpful for data centers. These days, most of the researchers are implementing bio-inspired methods for this energy crisis. Therefore, we have also used multi-objective optimization along with BPNN for the optimal placement of virtual machines over servers inside data centers.

We have proposed a BPGA and energy-aware model for VM placement to minimize the host usage. This model uses a divide and conquer approach for the optimal solution to this problem. The problem has been solved in two passes, where the first pass uses NSGA and the second pass uses BPNN for the most suitable VM placement.

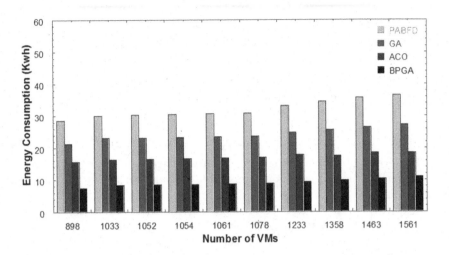

FIGURE 8.7   Energy consumption vs number of VMs (PlanetLab Trace).

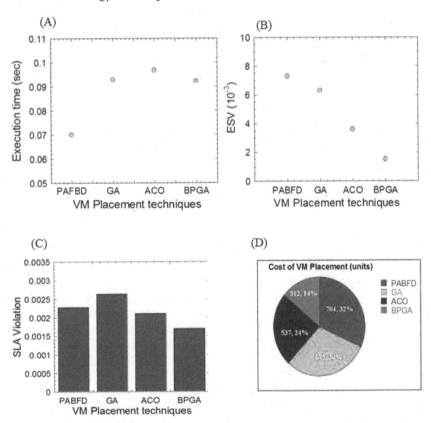

FIGURE 8.8   (a) energy consumption vs VM placement techniques, (b) ESV vs VM placement techniques, (c) SLA violations vs VM placement techniques and (d) cost of various VM placement techniques (PlanetLab Trace).

In this work, we have used CloudSim for the simulation of the proposed model; in future we would like to work on CloudStack which provides a real infrastructure. Moreover, considering the different network topology of data center, its network structures are also a few research directions where one can provide contributions.

REFERENCES

1. Md Hasanul Ferdaus, Manzur Murshed, "Energy-aware virtual machine consolidation in IaaS cloud computing", *Cloud Computing*, pp. 179–208, 2014.
2. Perspectives I, "Using a total cost of ownership (TCO) model for your data center", 2013. URL: http://www.datacenterknowledge.com/archives/2013/10/01/using-a-totalcost-of-ownership-tco-model-for-your-data-center/, last accessed: 02-01-2014.
3. Saurabh Kumar Garg, Srinivasa K. Gopalaiyengar, Rajkumar Buyya, "SLA-based resource provisioning for heterogeneous workloads in a virtualized cloud datacenter", in Proceedings of 11th International Conference on Algorithms and Architectures for Parallel Processing, pp. 371–384, 2011.
4. Nguyen QH, Nam T, Nguyen T, "Epobf: Energy efficient allocation of virtual machines in high performance computing cloud", *Journal of Science and Technology*, Vol. 51(4B), pp. 173–182, 2013.
5. Nakku K, Jungwook C, Euiseong S, "Energy-credit scheduler: An energy-aware virtual machine scheduler for cloud systems", *Future Generation Computer System*, Vol. 32, pp. 128–137, 2014.
6. Atefeh K, Saurabh K, Rajkumar B, "Energy and carbon-efficient placement of virtual machines in distributed cloud data centers", in *Euro-par 2013 Parallel Processing. Lecture Notes in Computer Science*, Vol. 80(97), Springer, Berlin, pp. 317–328, 2013.
7. Sheikh H, Tan H, Ahmad I, Ranka S, Bv P, "Energy- and performance-aware scheduling of tasks on parallel and distributed systems", *ACM Journal of Emerging Technology in Computing Systems*, Vol. 8(4), pp. 1–37, 2012.
8. George Kousiouris, Tommaso Cucinotta, Theodora Varvarigou, "The effects of scheduling, workload type and consolidation scenarios on virtual machine performance and their prediction through optimized artificial neural networks", *Journal of Systems and Software*, Vol. 84, pp. 1270–1291, 2011.
9. Haikun L, Hai J, Cheng X, Xiao L, "Performance and energy modeling for live migration of virtual machines", *Cluster Computing*, Vol. 16(2), pp. 249–264, 2013.
10. Zhang W, Song Y, Ruan L, "Resource management in internet-oriented data centers", *Journal of Software*, Vol.23(2), pp. 179–199, 2012.
11. Hongjian Li, Goufeng Zhu, Chenghuan Cui, Hong Tang, Yusheng Dou, Chen He, "Energy-efficient migration ans consolidation of virtual machines in data centers for cloud computing", *Journal of Computing*, Vol.98, pp. 303–317, 2016.

12. Fabio Lopez Pires, Benjamin Baran, "Multi-objective virtual machine placement with service level agreement: A Memetic algorithm, approach", In Proceedings of 6th International Conference on Utility and Cloud Computing, pp. 203–210, 2013.

13. Beloglazov A, Buyya R, "Optimal online deterministic algorithms and adaptive heuristics for energy and performance efficient dynamic consolidation of virtual machines in Cloud data centers", *Concurrency Computation: Practice and Experience*, Vol. 24, pp.1397–1420.2012.

14. Beloglazov A, Abawajy J, Buyya R, "Energy-aware resource allocation heuristics for efficient management of data centers for cloud computing", *Future Generation Computing System*, Vol. 28, pp. 755–68, 2012.

15. Ehsan Arianyan, Hassan Taheri, Saeed Sharifian, "Novel energy and SLA efficient resource management heuristics for consolidation of virtual machines in cloud data centers", *Computers and Electrical Engineering*, Vol. 47, pp. 222–240, 2015.

16. Buyya R, Ranjan R, Calheiros RN, "Modeling and simulation of scalable cloud computing environments and the cloudSim Toolkit: Challenges and opportunities", in Proceedings of the 7th High Performance Computing Simulation Conference (HPCS 2009), Leipzig, Germany, pp. 1–11, pp. 21–24. IEEE Press, New York, 2009.

17. Nathuji R, Schwan K, "Virtualpower: Coordinated power management in virtualized enterprise systems", *ACM SIGOPS Operating Systems Review*, Vol. 41(6), pp. 265–278, 2007.

18. Lim MY, Rawson F, Bletsch T, Freeh VW, "PADD: Power aware domain distribution", in Proceedings of the 29th IEEE International Conference on Distributed Computing Systems (ICDCS'09), Montreal, pp. 239–247, 2009.

19. Goiri I, Berral JL, Fit'o O, Juli`a F, Nou R, Guitart J, Gavalda R, Torres J, "Energy-efficient and multifaceted resource management for profit-driven virtualized data centers", *Future Generation Computer System*, Vol. 28(5), pp. 718–731, 2012.

20. Verma A, Ahuja P, Neogi A, "pMapper: Power and migration cost aware application placement in virtualized systems", in Proceedings of the 9th ACM/IFIP/USENIX International Conference on Middleware (Middleware'08), Leuven, Belgium, pp. 243–264. Springer, Berlin, 2008.

21. Verma A, Dasgupta G, Nayak T, De P, Kothari R, *Server Workload Analysis for Power Minimization Using Consolidation*, p. 28, USENIX Association, Berkeley, CA, 2009.

22. Ghribi C, Hadji M, Zeghlache D, "Energy efficient VM scheduling for cloud data centers: Exact allocation and migration algorithms', in Proceedings of 13th IEEE/ACM International Symposium on Cluster, Cloud, and Grid Computing, 2013. doi:10.1109/CCGrid.2013.89

23. Beloglazov A, Buyya R, "Energy efficient resource management in virtualized cloud data centers", in Proceedings of 10th IEEE/ACM International Conference on Cluster, Cloud and Grid Computing, pp. 826–831, 2010. doi:10.1109/CCGRID.2010.46

24. Beloglazov A, Buyya R, "Energy efficient allocation of virtual machines in cloud data centers", in 10th IEEE/ACM International Conference on Cluster, Cloud and Grid Computing (CCGrid), Melbourne, Australia, pp. 577–578, 2010.

25. A Anand, J Lakshmi, and SK Nandy, "Virtual machine placement optimization supporting performance SLAs", in Proceedings of the 5th IEEE International Conference on CloudComputing Technology and Science (CloudCom '13), Bristol, UK, pp. 298– 305, December 2013.

26. J Dong, H Wang, X Jin, Y Li, P Zhang, and S Cheng, "Virtual machine placement for improving energy efficiency and network performance in IaaS cloud", in Proceedings of the33rd IEEE International Conference on Distributed ComputingSystemsWorkshops (ICDCSW '13), IEEE, Philadelphia, PA, pp. 238–243, July 2013.

27. T Ferreto, CAF De Rose, H-U Heiss, "Maximum migration time guarantees in dynamic server consolidation for virtualized data centers", in *Euro-Par 2011 Parallel Processing, Vol. 6852 of Lecture Notes in Computer Science*, pp. 443–454, Springer, Berlin, Germany, 2011.

28. IS Moreno, R Yang, J Xu, T Wo, "Improved energy efficiency in cloud datacenters with interference-aware virtual machine placement", in Proceedings of the 11th IEEE InternationalSymposium on Autonomous Decentralized Systems(ISADS '13), IEEE, Mexico City, pp. 1–8, March 2013.

29. Sekhar J, Jeba G, "Energy efficient VM live migration in cloud data centers", *International Journal of Computer Science and Network*, Vol. 2(2), pp. 71–75, 2013.

30. Bila N, Lara ED, Joshi K, Lagar-Cavilla HA, Hiltunen M, Satyanarayanan M, "Jettison: Efficient idle desktop consolidation with partial vm migration", in Proceedings of the 7th ACM European Conference on Computer Systems. EuroSys '12, New York, pp. 211–224, 2012.

31. Zhou A, Wang S, Zheng Z, Hsu C, Lyu M, Yang F, "On cloud service reliability enhancement with optimal resource usage", in *IEEE Transactions on Cloud Computing*, vol. 99, pp. 1–1, 2014. doi:10.1109/TCC.2014.2369421.

32. Minas L, Ellison B, *Energy Efficiency for Information Technology: How to Reduce Power Consumption in Servers and Data Centers*, Intel press, 2009.

33. Nidhi Jain Kansal, Inderveer Chana, "Energy-aware virtual machine migration for cloud computing: A firefly optimization", *Journal of Grid Computing*, Vol. 14, pp. 327–345, 2016.

34. Khichar GD, Gupta G, Singh R, Rathi R "Maximum correlation with migration control based on modified knapsack (MC_MC) approach for VM selection for green cloud computing", in 8th International Conference on Cloud Computing, Data Science & Engineering, 2018.

35. Bajoria V, Katal A, Agarwal Y "An energy aware policy for mapping and migrating virtual machines in cloud environment using migration factor", in 8th International Conference on Cloud Computing, Data Science & Engineering, 2018.

36. Li Z, Shen H, Miles C, "PageRankVM: A pagerank based algorithm with anti-collocation constraints for virtual machine placement in cloud datacenters", in 38th International Conference on Distributed Computing Systems, 2018.

37. Maiyza AI, Hassan HA, Sheta WM, Sadek NM, Mokhtar MA, "And user's SLA-aware consolidation in cloud datacenters", in IEEE International Symposium on Signal Processing and Information Technology, 2017.

38. S Shen, VV Beek, A Iosup, "Statistical characterization of business-critical workloadshosted in cloud datacenters", in 15th IEEE/ACM International Symposium on Cluster,Cloud and Grid Computing, IEEE, pp.465–474, 2015.

39. X Fan, W Weber, L Barroso, "Power provisioning for a warehouse-sized computer", in Proceedings of the 34th Annual International Symposium on Computer Architecture, pp. 13–23, 2007.

40. SPEC power benchmarks, Standard Performance Evaluation Corporation, Retrieved from http://www.spec.org/benchmarks.html#power

41. Kumar D, Mishra KK, "Multi-objective optimization using co-variance guided Artificial Bee Colony", in *Journal of Information Science and Engineering*, Vol. 32, 2016.

42. Sharma O, Saini H, "VM consolidation for cloud data centers using median based threshold approach", in Proceedings of twelfth international multi-conference on information processing (IMCIP), Vol. 89, pp.27–33, 2016.

43. Sharma O, Saini H, "Energy efficient virtual machine consolidation for cloud datacenters using analytic hierarchy process", in *International Journal of Advanced Intelligence and Paradigms*, Vol. 10(4), pp. 401–422, 2018.

44. Caglar F, Shekhar S, Gokhale A, "iPlace: An intelligent and tunable power- and performance aware virtual machine placement technique for cloud – based real-time applications", in Proceedings of International Symposium on Object/Component/Service-Oriented Real-Time Distributed Computing, 2014.

45. Amazon elastic computing cloud (EC2), Retrieved from http://aws.amazon.com/ec2/instance-types

46. Park K, Pai VS, "CoMon: A mostly-scalable monitoring system for PlanetLab", *ACM SIGOPS Operating System Review*, Vol. 40, pp. 65–74, 2006.

CHAPTER 9

Meta-Heuristic Algorithms for Power Efficiency in Cloud Computing

Shally Vats, Sanjay Kumar Sharma and Sunil Kumar

CONTENTS

DOI: 10.1201/9781003185376-9

9.1 INTRODUCTION

The dream of using computing as a utility has come true with the emergence of cloud computing. Cloud allows you to use all the computing resources in the form of a variety of services [1]. All these services are very flexible which provides ease of use. In cloud computing cloud is metaphor for the Internet which means that the computing services can be acquired with the help of the Internet. As the Internet serves as the backbone of cloud computing all the services are location independent, i.e., to access the service you need an Internet connection and you can get access from anywhere in the world. There are numerous descriptions of cloud computing, but the standard definition is given by NIST [2]:

> Cloud computing is a model for enabling ubiquitous, convenient, on-demand network access to a shared pool of configurable computing resources (e.g. networks, servers, storage, applications, and services) that can be rapidly provisioned and released with minimal management effort or service provider interaction.

9.1.1 Essential Features of Cloud Computing

There are five essential characteristics of cloud computing, the presence of which makes a cloud system different from other computing environments like grid computing and distributed computing.

The Figure 9.1 shows those features of the cloud.

- **Measured services**: This feature allows the user to pay only for the service which is used by him. There is a metering capability in the cloud system which is used to measure the services provided to the

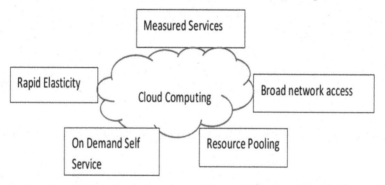

FIGURE 9.1   Characteristics of cloud computing. Figure 9.1 shows those features of the cloud. Characteristics of cloud computing are showcased in cloud.

users. Both the provider and users can monitor resource usage. Resource utilization is measured for each application so that billing can be done accordingly.

- **Rapid elasticity**: This feature makes the cloud services flexible in terms of their usage. The cloud services can be provisioned or released as per the requirements of the users. A rapid scale-up/down of the resources is needed for the better performance of the cloud system.

- **On-demand self-service**: This characteristic allows the cloud user to access the cloud services without the intervention of a cloud service provider. Web self-service can be used to demand the resources of the cloud data center. In cloud computing, a user can increase or decrease his service demands like storage, servers, etc., without human intervention.

- **Resource pooling**: Multi-tenancy is possible in the cloud due to this feature. In order to serve a large number of users a pool of resources is created in the cloud. The pool of these resources should be large enough and flexible to accommodate multiple tenants. Moreover, the cloud provides a level of abstraction to all the customers making the services independent of the physical location of resources.

- **Broad network access**: Cloud services can be accessed with its broad network around the world. These can be accessed through standard mechanisms which use heterogeneous thin or thick client platforms, e.g., workstations, laptops, tablets and mobile phones. This feature assures that no-one will go out of the loop in any case.

9.1.2 Cloud Service Models

Based upon the kind of services provided to the users the cloud can be divided into three service models. Figure 9.2 shows the service models.

- **Software as a service (SaaS)**: This is the model where software functionalities are provided through the Internet. A user accessing this model can be spared the installation of software and its maintenance. He can directly use any application with the help of an Internet browser. Google Docs is a very popular example of this.

- **Platform as a service (PaaS)**: The model has its utilization for application developers where they can directly start developing their applications

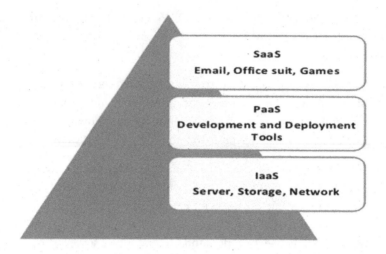

FIGURE 9.2   Cloud service models. Figure 9.2 shows the cloud service models in the real world.

without bothering about the installation of their working platform like operating system, server-side scripting language, etc. Google App Engine and Hadoop are very famous example of this model.

- **Infrastructure as a service (IaaS)**: Whenever anyone requires computing infrastructure like computing machines, network, storage, etc., then this model is used. All the resources are accessed by the users through virtualization. Google Compute Engine is an example of this kind of cloud model.

9.2 CLOUD TECHNOLOGY: VIRTUALIZATION

Provisioning separate resources to every user is not feasible in a cloud data center; hence it becomes necessary for the cloud service provider to introduce a mechanism to share the resources among multiple users without breaching their privacy. Virtualization is the solution for this. With the help of virtualization, the cloud service providers manage to accommodate a large number of users with less data center hardware. Virtualization creates various virtual machines that share the actual resources of the underlying physical machine. This is done with the help of a virtual machine monitor (VMM) which separates the computing environment and physical resources. Figure 9.3 demonstrates that multiple virtual machines can be created on a single hardware platform where all the VMs are completely isolated from each other. Cloud virtualization helps the cloud providers to give standard versions of their applications to the users. Virtualization

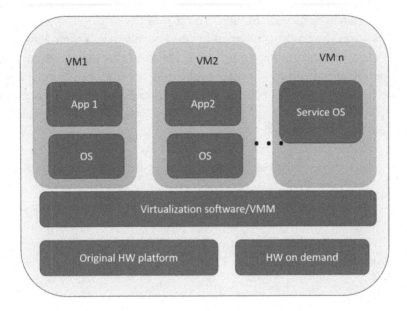

FIGURE 9.3 Virtualization in cloud. Figure 9.3 demonstrates that multiple virtual machines can be created on a single hardware platform where all the VMs are completely isolated from each other.

provides a uniform view of the resource pool of the cloud. The VMs are not dependent on the underlying hardware. VMM provides decoupling among VMs and PMs. It saves the state of the VM in a file. Hence a VM can be easily transferred from one PM to another PM just like a file. This characteristic plays an important role in cloud computing.

Virtualization is at the core of cloud computing. Every time a new request comes from the user a virtual machine is created to fulfill the request. With virtualization the users are isolated from each other.

9.2.1 Power Consumption in Cloud

The wide acceptability of cloud has increased the size of cloud enormously. Consequently the cloud data center consists of a large number of devices. IT infrastructure and its cooling system consume high amounts of power, which results in high electricity bills. The electricity bill is the major portion of operational cost. Every cloud provider tries to reduce his operational cost to achieve a high return on investment. Hence power management plays very crucial role in cloud because a major part of operation costs is due to power consumption. Among IT infrastructure, servers are the main consumers of power. In this chapter we will use the terms server and physical machine interchangeably. So most of the research work done so far considers the power consumed by servers only. All of them have used a linear power consumption model. It is observed that the growth of PM's CPU utilization from an idle state to the fully utilized state bears a linear relationship with energy consumption [3]. Therefore power consumption by a physical machine, P_{PM}, can be expressed in terms of its CPU utilization as shown in Equation 9.1.

$$P_{PM} = (p_{max} - p_{min}) \times U_{CPU} + p_{min} \qquad (9.1)$$

Where p_{max} is the power consumption at maximum workload and p_{min} is the power consumption at minimum workload where workload can be 0. It is observed that the idle server consumes 70% of energy [3]. So Equation 9.1 can be modified as shown in Equation 9.2.

$$P_{PM} = (0.3 \times U_{CPU} + 0.7) \times p_{max} \qquad (9.2)$$

In the same way power consumed by VM can be calculated. The prudent placement of VMs on servers can save power very efficiently. Low resource utilization contributes to power consumption [4]. It has been observed that most of the time the utilization of the servers of the cloud data center remains between 10% and 50% [5]. So the servers remain underutilized or idle for most of the time. It has been recorded that even an idle server consumes 70% of the power it consumes at peak load [3]. Therefore the idle servers can be switched off to save the power. VM consolidation is the most famous method of this type to save the energy consumed by underutilized servers in the cloud data center.

9.2.2 Virtual Machine Consolidation

In virtual machine consolidation, the utilization of servers is optimized. The idle PMs are switched off. VM consolidation tries to allocate a number of VMs to the minimum number of PMs. Using VM consolidation, the cloud service provider can achieve optimized utilization of its resources. In VM consolidation, VMs are relocated from one PM to another for the optimum use of resources. This contributes to dynamic resource management. When VMs are consolidated on the minimum number of PMs, then idle PMs can be switched off to save energy. The process of VM consolidation is shown in Figure 9.4.

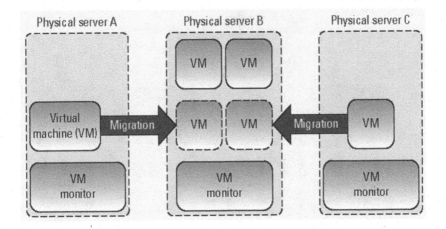

FIGURE 9.4 VM consolidation process. The process of VM consolidation is shown in Figure 9.4 for resource allocation in cloud infrastructure.

9.3 META-HEURISTIC ALGORITHMS FOR VM PLACEMENT

The task of VM placement is considered as NP-hard, so the optimal solution can't be found. Optimal placement of VMs is always a challenging task for the CSPs. Meta-heuristic algorithms can help a lot in this direction. Using these, one can get the solution which is near to optimal. A meta-heuristic is a high-level problem-independent algorithmic framework that provides a set of guidelines or strategies to develop heuristic optimization algorithms. Meta-heuristic algorithms are inspired by the solution to real-life problems. Depending upon the number of solutions the meta-heuristic algorithms can be broadly categorized into two types which are shown in Figure 9.5.

- **Single solution-based**: In this type of meta-heuristic approach only one candidate solution is taken. The heuristic applied tries to improve that solution only. Typical examples of this kind of meta-heuristic include simulated annealing and guided local search.

- **Population-based**: This considers a number of candidate solutions in the search space and tries to modify multiple solutions at a time. Ant colony optimization, particle swarm optimization and genetic algorithms are the famous examples of this.

9.3.1 Simulated Annealing

This is a technique which is used to optimize the function in a large search space. It is inspired by physical annealing where a material is heated and cooled down to convert it into the desired structure. The process starts

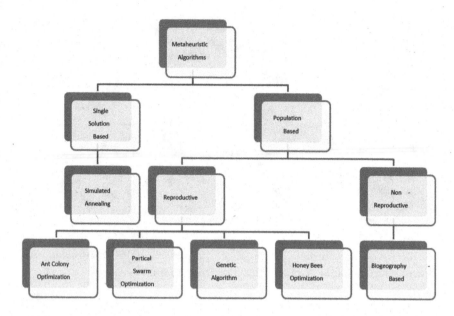

FIGURE 9.5 Categorization of meta-heuristic algorithms. The figure shows the categorization of various existing meta-heuristic algorithms for task scheduling in cloud infrastructure.

with some random solution termed the initial solution. At this time temperature is set to T_0. There are three temperature reduction rules, namely: Linear reduction, slow decrease and geometric reduction. Any one of the three can be taken depending upon the model that is being used. Temperature is reduced iteratively till the termination condition is reached. Then a neighboring solution is taken and considered as the new solution. If the difference in cost function of the old solution and the new solution is more than 1 then the new solution is better, otherwise the older one. The process continues till the termination condition is reached.

Algorithm: Simulated Annealing
```
    Take a random solution Soln₀
    Set Temperature = T₀,
    While (Termination condition not reached) do
       Reduce the temperature
       Find a neighbor Soln₁ of Soln₀
       If (fitness(Soln₁) is better than fitness(Soln₀))
              Soln₀=Soln₁
    end while return
    Soln₀
```

Wu et al. [6] were the first to apply simulated annealing to find the optimal placement of VMs in a cloud data center to save energy. The name of the proposed method is simulated annealing based virtual machine placement (SAVMP). The method is divided into four parts. The first part finds a placement configuration for VMs on PMs with some constraints. A neighbor configuration of the initial configuration is generated. Then in the third part, the deviation in energy for the new configuration is calculated. In the last part temperature scheduling is done. The method was compared with FFD, and it was found that SAVMP consumed less energy.

Rajabzadeh et al. [7] proposed a VM management method. It uses parallel simulated annealing in a Markov chain model for VM placement. There are two managers called the global manager and local manager. The global manager takes care of VM migration and consolidation whereas the local manager detects overload/underload/critical conditions and selects VM for migration. Where initial placement is. The critical condition occurs when the major portion of the main memory is occupied because it may lead to SLA violations. The initial population consists of a list of PMs excluding low-loaded and overloaded PMs which is done using the interquartile range. Then the VMs to be migrated are taken into consideration with a condition that the number of VMs should be the same as the number of PMs present in the list. Initially a random allocation scheme is taken and its fitness value is calculated. A fitness function calculates the increase in energy consumption after the placement of particular VM. Initial temperature is set to T_0. The authors have designed their own model to set the initial temperature. A number of neighbors are generated for each member of the population, and their fitness value is calculated. According to the SA comparison rule every member of the population is compared with its neighbor and if a neighbor wins then it is added to the primary population. The process is iterated till the termination condition is reached. The work is simulated on CloudSim and compared with LRMMT and LRMC [8]. It is found to perform better than the compared algorithms.

Marotta et al. [9] have proposed a VM consolidation method based on simulated annealing. They have taken a set j of PMs. And set m of VMs. The problem is defined as with the given set of VMs allocated to a set of PMs, there is a need to find the migration scheme of VMs so that the linear combination of power consumed by the new set of active PMs and the number of migrations is minimum. The algorithm consists of a perturbation phase where with the current solution a new solution is found

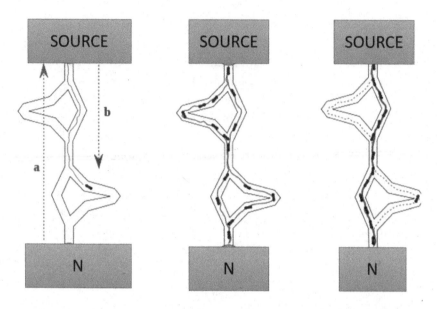

FIGURE 9.6 Ant colony optimization. During the process the ants identify the shortest path between the two as shown in the figure. There are two paths to reach the food in Figure 9.6. Based upon the pheromone present on the path all the ants select the shorter path to the food.

by the migration of a single VM known as perturbing. The VM migration is done using a desirability index which is the sigmoid function of VM's utilization. The algorithm was compared with FFD and Sercon [10], and it consumed less power when implemented in Java.

9.3.2 Ant Colony Optimization

The ant colony algorithm is a probabilistic technique used for optimization problems. It was introduced by Marco Dorigo in the 1990s. It is based upon the foraging behavior of the ant in search of a path between the food and its colony. During the process the ants identify the shortest path between the two as shown in Figure 9.6. There are two paths to reach the food in Figure 9.6. Based upon the pheromone present on the path all the ants select the smaller path to the food at time $T = 3$.

Algorithm: Ant Colony Optimization
```
Generate a number of solutions (ants) termed as
population Initialize pheromone trail and
parameter
Position each ant on starting node
```

```
While (Termination condition not reached) do
         Repeat for each
         ant a do
         Choose next node by state transition
         rule Update pheromone end for
    Until every ant has a solution
    Update best
  solution end while return
  best solution
```

X. F. Liu et al. [11] have proposed a method for virtual machine placement using the ant colony algorithm. On combining the method with order exchange migration it is called OEMACS. It has considered two resources, i.e., CPU and memory, for checking the capacity of the PM for the allocation of VM. Power consumption is calculated for CPU only. The adjacency matrix is used to get the mapping of VMs and PMs. ACO finds the mapping of VMs to PMs such that the number of PMs in active state is minimum to optimize power consumption. The pheromone consists of information regarding the relationship among the VMs. The criterion of consolidating VMs is to allocate related VMs on the same PM. Initially the VM and PM have one-to-one mapping. In each iteration the number of PMs is decreased with the solution generated using pheromones. Order exchange operation is used to balance the resource utilization of PMs, i.e., VM migration from overloaded PMs. The result shows that the proposed algorithm performs very well in homogeneous as well as heterogeneous environments.

Aryania et al. [12] proposed an energy-aware VM consolidation based on an ant colony system (EVMCACS). It considers two resources: CPU and memory for categorizing the PMs into four types, namely normal-loaded, low-load, high-load and predicted high-load. During the consolidation of VM, it takes into consideration the energy consumed in migrating the VM too, which is approximated as a function of VM size. The proposed algorithm was compared with ACSVMC [13] and found to be better than the compared one where performance is evaluated in terms of the number of PMs powered off, the number of VM migrations and SLA violation.

Fares et al. [14] have designed a VM placement method to reduce the power consumption of the data center. In their work they have proposed a new heuristic embedded in ant colony optimization to place VMs on PMs. The method takes a solution of first fit decreasing [14] as the value of the initial pheromone. The heuristic which identifies the best PM for a particular VM takes account of not only power consumption but CPU utilization and CPU capacity too. The algorithm works in two modules. The first one finds the best solution for each ant, and the second tries to improve the global best solution. The method is evaluated on three parameters, viz, energy saving, scalability and runtime performance. The method was compared with two existing algorithms, and the results show that it is better than the compared algorithms.

9.3.3 Particle Swarm Optimization

Particle swarm optimization was designed by Kennedy in 1995. This is a population-based stochastic algorithm. It is based upon the behavior of a fish school or a flock of birds. In the optimization problem, a swarm is the set of candidate solutions. The single potential solution is termed as particle. A particle has two characteristics, i.e., position and velocity. The particles can interact with each other to find the best solution. Every particle has a fitness value which is calculated using objective function. Each particle knows its own best performance and the best performance of the swarm. Based upon the best, each particle changes its velocity and accordingly the position changes. The figure shows that initially the bird was flying in a different direction and it changes its direction according to the global best (Figure 9.7).

The pseudo code describes the general procedure of particle swarm algorithm to achieve the optimized value of any function.

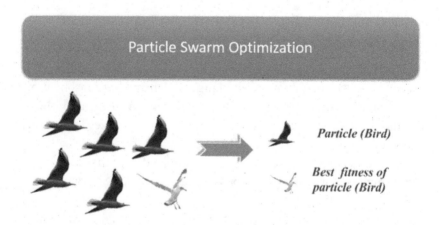

FIGURE 9.7 Particle swarm optimization. The figure shows that initially the bird was flying in a different direction and it changes its direction according to global best using particle swarm optimization.

Algorithm: Particle Swarm Optimization

```
      Initialize particles with random position and
      velocity.
      While (Termination condition not reached) do
   for each particle p do
         Calculate fitness(p)
   if( fitness(p) is better than best(p) )
   set best(p) = fitness(p)          end if
   if( best(p) is better than gbest
   gbest = best(p)          end for
            for each particle p do
   update position and velocity of p
            end for
   end while
            return
   gbest
```

Xiong et al. [15] have proposed a VM placement algorithm for energy optimization based upon particle swarm optimization named multi-resource energy efficiency based on particle swarm optimization (MREE-PSO). There are n number of VMs and m number of PMs. The particles are the VMs. The position vector of particles is defined as $X^t_i = (x^t_{i1}, x^t_{i2}, ..., x^t_{ij}, ..., x^t_{im})$, where t denotes the number of iterations, i represents the ith possible solution and j is the sequence number of VM. The position is updated for all the particles with the help of an $m*n$ 0-1 matrix. The entry will be 1 if the particular VM is allocated to the specified PM, otherwise 0. P_{best} and G_{best} are the vectors for personal best and global best. The values of the personal and global fitness functions are set to 0.8 and 0.7 to avoid the local optima. The iterations are stopped when they reach a predefined number. The mapping found in the last iteration is considered as the final VM placement on PMs. The algorithm is simulated on CloudSim and found to be energy efficient compared with the algorithms.

Aruna et al. [16] have proposed particle swarm optimization for the placement of VMs on PMs where the objective was to minimize power consumption. They have used a linear power model of CPU for the calculation of power consumption. They have taken N number of VMs and M number of PMs based on condition $N < M$. So the particle has N dimensional vector. Each dimension can be mapped to a set of discrete values limited to M. Each particle is assigned a random position and velocity initially. The current position of each particle is termed as personal best. The fitness function is the sum energy consumption of each particle that is to be minimized. Depending upon the personal best and global best the position and velocity of each particle are updated using the general equation of position and velocity update. Thus iteratively the goal of finding a placement of VMs so that the power consumption of PMs used is minimum is achieved. The algorithm was simulated on CloudSim and found better than a non-power-aware method.

Ibrahim et al. [17] proposed a power-aware technique depending on particle swarm optimization (PAPSO) to determine the near-optimal placement for the migrated VMs. The technique not only tries to reduce the power consumption of the PMs, but it takes care of SLA violations too. This is done by keeping the number of overloaded PMs as low as possible. The process considers the set of PMs excluding overloaded PMs and the set of VMs to be migrated. The mapping is generated and its fitness value is calculated. The technique is implemented on CloudSim and compared with power-aware best fit decreasing. It is found better in terms of energy consumption as well as SLA violations.

9.3.4 Genetic Algorithm

The genetic algorithm is a heuristic for search which is based on Charles Darwin's theory of natural evolution. The genetic algorithm progresses in five phases, namely: Initial population, fitness function, selection, crossover and mutation. A set of individuals is considered as the initial population. All individuals have defined parameters called genes. The genes undergo mutation and crossover to produce a better next generation. The produced individual is tested with a fitness function and the best individuals are selected for reproduction. Thus by iterating them we get the best individual of the next generation, and we stop after we reach the goal.

```
Algorithm: Genetic Algorithm
        Generate population with random individuals
        While ( Termination condition not reached ) do
        for each individual i do
        Calculate fitness(i)
        end for
        Select best individuals
        Apply crossover on selected individuals
        Apply mutation on selected individuals
        Update population with better
individuals      end while      return best individuals
```

Tang et al. [18] have proposed a hybrid genetic algorithm (HGA) to place VMs in a power-efficient way. The process considers the energy consumed by PMs as well as the communication network of the PMs. It has used a three-tier architecture for PMs. The goal is to minimize the energy consumption of PMs as well as communication taking place between VMs. There are some feasibility conditions like the CPU and memory capacity of the PMs. The process takes each individual from the population and checks for feasibility conditions. If it does not qualify then a repair procedure is applied to make it feasible and its fitness value is calculated. In order to pair an individual solution, a roulette selection procedure is applied. To produce the offspring biased uniform crossover is used. The process continues till the best solution is found. The work is implemented in Java and found better than the genetic algorithm.

Zhao et al. [19] proposed a novel VM placement algorithm which combines genetic algorithm and Tabu search algorithm, collectively called GATA. In the work, there is a set V denoting the set of VMs and H denotes the set of PMs (hosts). The objective is to find a set $H' \subseteq H$ such that it can host all the existing VMs such that power consumption by the PMs in H' is minimum and load is balanced to meet QoS. The VM placement scheme is represented by equallength-real-coding. If there is n number of VMs and m number of PMs considering $n < m$, then initially the population is random allocation of VMs to PMs such that only one VM is allocated to one PM. So the process will stop when m^{min} is reached.

9.3.5 Biogeographic-Based Optimization (BBO)

Biogeography is the study of the distribution of species in geographical space. It was proposed by Simon in 2008. It studies the migration of species among different habitats where each habitat is associated with a habitat suitability index (HSI). HSI is based on suitability index variables (SIVs). The habitat with high HSI has a high rate of emigration and low rate of immigration. In optimization each candidate solution is termed as a habitat. The fitness value of the candidate solution is its HSI. The major difference between this and GA is that it does not involve reproduction.

```
Algorithm: Biogeographic-Based Optimization
        Generate a random set of habitats
         For each habitat H_i do
        Calculate HSI_i of each habitat. end
        for
```

```
         Arrange habitats in ascending order of their HSI
          While (termination condition not reached)
             Update species count for each habitat
                Calculate immigration and emigration
                rate of all habitats
             Apply migration and mutation to get updated
             set of habitats of solutions
end while
          return best solution
```

Zheng et al. [20] have proposed a multi-objective VM placement method based on BBO named VMPMBBO. Their aim in VM placement is to minimize energy consumption as well resource wastage with a constraint that the requirement for resources of a hosted VM on a particular PM will not exceed the resources of that PM. The method is compared with three existing multi-objective methods and found better when simulation is performed on synthetic data.

Liu, Jialei et al. [21] mapped the virtual machine placement problem to an ecosystem model and redefined the original BBO algorithm operators. The modified BBO policy is tested for robustness, performance and scalability. The ecosystem model is simulated on WebCloudSim. The performance is compared with RFF, SGGA-P, SBBO-R and MGGA.

9.3.6 Honey Bee Optimization

Honey bee optimization algorithm was designed by Pham, Ghanbarzadeh et al. in 2005 [22]. It is based on the foraging behavior of honey bees. A segment of bees called scout bees are in search of good food from flowers. In an optimization problem each candidate solution is considered as a food source and a population of bees is used to search in the solution space for the best solution.

Algorithm: Honey Bee Optimization
```
Initialize with random population
While (termination condition not reached) do
        Employ scout bees in search of food.
        Convert scout bees to employed bees.
         Calculate the amount of nectar from employed bees.
         If (onlooker bees are distributed)        then
        select food source for onlooker and its
        neighbor.
         else
```

```
Memorize best position
Find the exhausted food source and convert
employed bees into scout bees. end if
end while
return best food position
```

P. Sharma et al. [23] have proposed a task scheduling technique using the honey bee algorithm. The designed method is for mobile cloud computing where a mobile user sends a request for processing to the cloud server. First they have applied modified best fit decreasing to sort the tasks. The artificial bee algorithm is combined with support vector machine to optimize task scheduling and reduce the energy consumption. The work is tested on MATLAB® and compared with existing methods in [24]. The result shows that the proposed method is more energy efficient.

Liu et al. [25] proposed an energy-efficient virtual machine migration strategy in mobile cloud. They proposed two models, namely a virtual machine task model and an energy model where they have described the characteristics of VMs and energy consumed by the PMs respectively. The VM migration system consists of two parts, the host group and migration controller. The migration controller runs an artificial bee algorithm after the user requests passes sound monitor. The proposed method was simulated on CloudSim and found energy efficient.

9.3.7 Bat Optimization

Bat optimization was designed by Xin-She Yang in 2010. It is based upon the echolocation behavior of bats with a varying pulse rate of emission and loudness. All bats use echolocation to sense distance, and they also 'know' the difference between food/prey and background barriers. Bats fly randomly with velocity v_i at position x_i with a fixed frequency f_{min} (or wavelength λ), varying wavelength λ (or frequency f) and loudness A_0 to search for prey. They can automatically adjust the wavelength (or frequency) of their emitted pulses and adjust the rate of pulse emission $r \in$ [0,1], depending on the proximity of their target. Although the loudness can vary in many ways, we assume that the loudness varies from a large (positive) A_0 to a minimum value A_{min}.

```
Bat Optimization
Initialize the bat population with x_i and v_i (i = 1,2,...,n)
Define frequency of f_i at x_i
```

```
Initialize pulse rates r_i and the loudness A_i
While (Termination condition not reached) do
Generate new solutions by adjusting frequency and
update velocities and positions.
If (rand > r_i)
    Select a solution among the best solutions
    randomly;
    Generate a local solution around the selected best
    solution by a local random  walk
end if
If (rand < A_i and fitness(x_i) < fitness(x_cgbest))
    Accept the new solution
    Increases r_i and decrease A_i
end if
Rank the bats in each iteration and store their
current global best x_cgbest end while return best
solution
```

Y. Gu et al. [26] have proposed an energy-aware, time and throughput optimization heuristic (EATTO) method for workflow scheduling. It is based upon bat optimization. The tasks are arranged according to their computational requirement and precedence constraint. Each mapping of the tasks is considered a bat. The solution is evaluated at each generation t using the following metrics: A frequency or wavelength fb^t_i, a velocity v^t_i, a loudness A^t_i, a pulse emission rate r^t_i and a location d^t_i. The loudness A^t_i and pulse emission rates $r^t i$ can be varied during the iterations. For the purpose of simplicity, we use the definitions $A^i_{t+1} = \alpha A^i_t$ and $r^i_{t+1} = r^0_i [1 - \exp(-\gamma t)]$, where $0 < \alpha < 1$ and $\gamma > 0$ are two constants. Initially a random population of bats is generated with specified parameters and the current best is calculated. With random walk a new population is generated and local search is performed to get the best solution and the process goes on till the termination condition is met. The performance was measured using different parameters like energy consumption, task completion time and energy efficiency cost and found better in all terms.

Raghavan S. et al. [27] proposed a binary bat algorithm for scheduling workflow in a cloud. The algorithm is used to map the tasks and resources. The mapping is done based on the total cost of computation. Only the cost of processing is considered as computing cost. The performance is compared with best resource selection (BRS) algorithm. The cost for the proposed algorithm is less than the BRS for the set of four tasks.

TABLE 9.1 Meta-Heuristic Algorithms Comparative Analysis

Meta-Heuristic Approach	Prominent Contributions in Literature	Salient Points	Limitations
Simulated annealing	[6, 7, 9]	• Significant improvement in energy consumption [6]. • Energy consumption is reduced with SLA requirements [7]. • Simulated annealing is used in Markov chain model for VM placement [7]. • Mixed integer programming model is proposed with simulated annealing-based heuristic [9].	• Performance is only compared with first fit decreasing algorithm [6]. • Energy consumed by switching devices not considered [7]. • Performance not checked on real-time data [7]. • Energy consumed by networking devices not considered [9].
Ant colony optimization	[11–14]	• Performs better on VMP in bottleneck resource characteristics [11]. • Energy consumed during VM migration is considered. • Performance is improved on multiple parameters [12]. • Works on live VM migration and satisfies the QoS requirements [13]. • Reduction in energy consumption with good scalability [14].	• Network cost is not considered [11]. • Energy consumption model during VM migration is too simplistic [12]. • Experiments are not conducted on real-world cloud environment [13]. • Run time is on higher side [14].
Particle swarm optimization	[15–17]	• Energy consumption and resource utilization collectively addressed using Euclidean distance from the optimal point [15]. • A power model for servers is proposed [16]. • Discrete version of particle swarm optimization based on decimal encoding is used for the optimal VM placement [17].	• Performance comparison is performed only with MBFD and MFBH [15]. • Comparative analysis is not exhaustive [16]. • Comparative analysis not exhaustive [17].

(*Continued*)

TABLE 9.1 (Continued) Meta-Heuristic Algorithms Comparative Analysis

Meta-Heuristic Approach	Prominent Contributions in Literature	Salient Points	Limitations
Genetic algorithm	[18, 19]	• Energy consumption by communication network is considered using hybrid genetic algorithm [18]. • Genetic algorithm is combined with Tabu search for reducing energy consumption, and load balancing [19].	• HGA is not tested with energy consumption but the communication network [18]. • Execution time is on higher side [19].
Biogeographic-based optimization	[20, 21]	• Minimize both energy consumption and resource wastage. Superior adaptability and extensibility [20]. • New ecosystem model is proposed [21].	• Performance comparison is limited [20]. • Time taken for successive generations increases rapidly with increase in number of VMs [21].
Honey bee optimization	[23, 25]	• SVM is used along with ABC algorithm to reduce energy consumption in mobile cloud computing [23]. • Higher QoS with a smaller number of failed VM requests [25].	• Comparative analysis is not on all related parameters [23]. • Only compared with GA and RM strategies [25].
Bat optimization	[26, 27]	• Energy aware, time and throughput optimization [26]. • Workflow optimization is done for overall cost reduction using binary bat algorithm [27].	• Comparison is not on standard data [26]. • Performance comparison is not exhaustive [27].

9.4 CONCLUSION

Meta-heuristic algorithms have played a significant role in the optimization of resources and hence saving energy in the operation of cloud data centers. Different types of meta-heuristic algorithms have been tried by researchers for reducing the energy consumption. The algorithms have been applied on VM placement for achieving machine consolidation. However, they are not the solution for every scenario. Hence, there is a need to identify the suitability of a particular meta-heuristic algorithm. The chapter has provided a reasonable insight into the prominent contributions in the literature in the area of meta-heuristic algorithms in energy-efficient operations of cloud data centers. Table 9.1 presents a comparative view of the existing meta-heuristic algorithms proposed to reduce the energy consumption. In most of the research, energy consumed by network devices is not considered. Also, the comparative analysis in most cases is not exhaustive. Hence, further work can be pursued to address these issues.

REFERENCES

1. R. M. Al-Dwairi, N. Al-Tweit, and K. Zyout, "Factors influencing cloud-computing adoption in small and medium E-commerce enterprises in Jordan," *ACM Int. Conf. Proc. Ser.*, vol. 16, no. 1, pp. 73–78, 2018.
2. P. Mell and T. Grance, "The NIST definition of cloud computing," *NIST Spec. Publ.*, vol. 145, p. 7, 2011.
3. X. Fan, W.-D. Weber, and L. A. Barroso, "Power provisioning for a warehouse-sized computer," in Proceedings of the 34th Annual International Symposium on Computer Architecture - ISCA '07, 2007, vol. 35, no. 2, pp. 13–23.
4. A. Beloglazov, R. Buyya, Y. C. Lee, and A. Zomaya, *A Taxonomy and Survey of Energy-Efficient Data Centers and Cloud Computing Systems*, 1st ed., vol. 82. Elsevier Inc., 2011.
5. A. Barroso, Luiz and H. Urs, "The case for energy-proportional computing," *Case Energy-Proportional Comput.*, vol. 40, no. 12, pp. 33–37, 2007.
6. Y. Wu, M. Tang, and W. Fraser, "A simulated annealing algorithm for energy efficient virtual machine placement," in Conference Proceedings - IEEE International Conference on Systems, Man and Cybernetics, 2012, pp. 1245–1250.
7. M. Rajabzadeh and A. T. Haghighat, "Energy-aware framework with Markov chain-based parallel simulated annealing algorithm for dynamic management of virtual machines in cloud data centers," *J. Supercomput.*, vol. 73, no. 5, pp. 2001–2017, 2017.
8. A. Beloglazov and R. Buyya, "Optimal online deterministic algorithms and adaptive heuristics for energy and performance efficient dynamic consolidation of virtual machines in cloud data centers," *Concurr. Comput. Pract. Exp.*, vol. 24, no. 13, pp. 1397–1420, 2012.

9. A. Marotta and S. Avallone, "A simulated annealing based approach for power efficient virtual machines consolidation," in Proceedings - 2015 IEEE 8th International Conference on Cloud Computing, CLOUD 2015, 2015, pp. 445–452.

10. A. Murtazaev and S. Oh, "Sercon: server consolidation algorithm using live migration of virtual machines for green computing," *IETE Tech. Rev.*, vol. 28, no. 3, pp. 212–231, 2011.

11. X. F. Liu, Z. H. Zhan, J. D. Deng, Y. Li, T. Gu, and J. Zhang, "An energy efficient ant colony system for virtual machine placement in cloud computing," *IEEE Trans. Evol. Comput.*, vol. 22, no. 1, pp. 113–128, 2018.

12. A. Aryania, H. S. Aghdasi, and L. M. Khanli, "Energy-aware virtual machine consolidation algorithm based on ant colony system," *J. Grid Comput.*, vol. 16, no. 3, pp. 477–491, 2018.

13. F. Farahnakian et al., "Using ant colony system to consolidate vms for green cloud computing," *IEEE Trans. Serv. Comput.*, vol. 8, no. 2, pp. 187–198, 2014.

14. F. Alharbi, Y. C. Tian, M. Tang, W. Z. Zhang, C. Peng, and M. Fei, "An ant colony system for energy-efficient dynamic virtual machine placement in data centers," *Expert Syst. Appl.*, vol. 120, pp. 228–238, 2019.

15. Xiong, A. P. and C. X. Xu, "Energy efficient multiresource allocation of virtual machine based on PSO in cloud data center," *Math. Probl. Eng.*, vol. 2014, pp. 1–12, 2014.

16. P. Aruna and S. Vasantha, "A particle swarm optimization algorithm for power-aware virtual machine allocation," in 6th International Conference on Computing, Communications and Networking Technologies, ICCCNT 2015, 2015, pp. 1–6.

17. A. Ibrahim, M. Noshy, H. A. Ali, and M. Badawy, "PAPSO: A power-aware VM placement technique based on particle swarm optimization," *IEEE Access*, vol. 8, pp. 81747–81764, 2020.

18. M. Tang and S. Pan, "A hybrid genetic algorithm for the energy-efficient virtual machine placement problem in data centers," *Neural Process. Lett.*, vol. 41, no. 2, pp. 211–221, 2015.

19. D. M. Zhao, J. T. Zhou, and K. Li, "An energy-aware algorithm for virtual machine placement in cloud computing," *IEEE Access*, vol. 7, pp. 55659–55668, 2019.

20. Z. Qinghua, L. Rui, and X. L, "Virtual machine consolidated placement based on multiobjective biogeography-based optimization," in 15th IEEE/ACM Intl. Symp. on Cluster, Cloud and Grid Computing, 2015, pp. 687–696.

21. Liu, Jialei, Wang, Shangguang, Zhou, Ao, & Yang, Fangchun "A virtual machine placement policy via biogeography-based optimization in the cloud," in IMCOM '18: Proceedings of the 12th International Conference on Ubiquitous Information Management and Communication, 2018, vol. 54, pp 1–8. 10.1145/3164541.3164553.

22. E. Koc et al., "Bee algorithm a novel approach to function optimisation," *Manuf. Eng. Cent.*, vol. 0501, no. September, pp. 1–12, 2005.

23. Sharma P., Kumari R., and Aulakh I.K. "Task-aware energy-efficient framework for mobile cloud computing," in Tuba M., Akashe S., Joshi A. (eds) *ICT Systems and Sustainability. Advances in Intelligent Systems and Computing*, 2020, vol 1077. Springer.

24. S. Guo, J. Liu, Y. Yang, B. Xiao, and Z. Li, "Energy-efficient dynamic computation offloading and cooperative task scheduling in mobile cloud computing," *IEEE Trans. Mob. Comput.*, vol. 18, no. 2, pp. 319–333, 2019.

25. Y. Liu, P. Fan, J. Zhu, L. Wen, and X. Fan, "High-efficient energy saving processing of big data of communication under mobile cloud computing," *Int. J. Model. Simulation, Sci. Comput.*, vol. 10, no. 4, pp. 1–11, 2019.

26. Y. Gu and C. Budati, "Energy-aware workflow scheduling and optimization in clouds using bat algorithm," *Futur. Gener. Comput. Syst.*, vol. 113, pp. 106–112, 2020.

27. Raghavan, S., Sarwesh, P., Marimuthu, C., and Chandrasekaran, K., "Bat algorithm for scheduling workflow applications in cloud," in 2015 International Conference on Electronic Design, Computer Networks & Automated Verification (EDCAV), 2015.

CHAPTER 10

Intelligent Scalable Algorithm for Resource Efficiency in Cloud

Arjun Singh, Punit Gupta, Vijay Kumar Sharma, Tarun Jain and Surbhi Chauhan

CONTENTS

10.1 INTRODUCTION

In the previous few years, cloud computing has revolutionized the world from data-access devices to devices that are capable of processing and storing giant quantities of data. Cloud computing is designed for growing the cloud offerings on hand and available anytime, anywhere from cell

DOI: 10.1201/9781003185376-10

devices. The cloud customers can make use of the limited resources of cellular devices. Mostly, the current cloud environments do not now reflect on consideration of the cellular devices. Clouds are truly pervasive and nomadic for the subsequent generation. Hence the integration of cloud is critical to have an effect on available resources and widen the variety of services furnished. Cloud units are confined to processing power, battery existence and storage capacity. These constraints lead to sluggish utility execution and reduce operability. Devices in the cloud environment might also behave as consumers of cloud structure assets or as framework source providers. Their integration into the cloud or cluster as useful resource vendors (not simply as consumers) is very difficult due to the various constraints on the electricity and processing capability of cell devices. There are three techniques for the integration of devices into the cloud:

a) The cellular units are simply the interfaces to sources available in the cloud system, and do not supply any services.

b) Raw assets like CPU, memory and storage in cellular units are used to end the duties in the cloud environment. This scheme simply considers cellular units as traditional sources to achieve goals.

c) This scheme is to boost offerings in cell units to help the cellular offerings in a cellular cloud and to enable cell units to furnish services. This mannequin is the one that contributes the most whole integration in which the cell units can be both customers and carriers of services. Such integration could open up possibilities in growing the cell nature of these devices in a cloud computing environment.

A dispensed computing infrastructure that is used to solve difficult scientific and engineering issues is termed a cloud. It is differentiated from traditional disbursed computing structures in its large-scale aid sharing and revolutionary applications. Conglomerations of countless assets with distinct proprietors are computational clouds. Recently, this structure has been superior to control a number of cell units in order to offer a seamless supply of computational strength and storage capacity. Load balancing or job scheduling difficulty is the environmentally friendly allocation of jobs and utilization of sources of unused devices, which is a fundamental consideration of such cloud computing systems. The job allocator assigns the jobs to the accessible sources and tries to optimize a distinct overall performance metric, for example, time cut-off date or income maximization [1–4].

10.2 ENERGY-CONSTRAINED CLOUD INFRASTRUCTURE

Restricted battery capability will become a constraint and electricity or strength administration will become a problem when the assets are cloud-based. As the devices are heterogeneous, battery ability can also additionally be heterogeneous. To maximize the overall performance and the cost effectiveness of the system, the heterogeneity of the sources and duties in an HC machine is developed [5–7]. A sizeable lookup difficulty is how to allocate resources to the duties and to order the duties for execution on the resources to expand some overall performance criterion of a cellular cloud which is called mapping or aid allocation. Useful resource allocation will pay interest in allocating assets on a certain device [8–10].

This chapter realizes some parameters and assets to supply an answer for aid administration and make it energy efficient. Finally, an appropriate calculation is accomplished for a similar method and then a min-max algorithm and scheduled resource are offered.

To grant higher understanding, this chapter offers an appropriate introduction in Section 10.1 that is accompanied by way of the existing work's description current in area two. Then the chapter describes the problem and offers the best answer for the problem in Section 10.3. Finally, the chapter offers a conclusion in the last section.

10.3 LITERATURE REVIEW

Li Chunlin et al. [11] have proposed fee-based totally dispensed strength confined aid allocation optimization for cell clouds which is formulated as a utility optimization problem. This difficulty can be decomposed into two sub-problems. The interplay between the two sub-problems is managed with the aid of the use of a pricing variable. The utility is primarily based on its allotted resources which include computation and communication assets and on the electricity used which motivates a coupled utility model. In this model, the utilities are the features of allotted resources and energy consumed. Abdul Aziz et al. [12] have proposed quite a number of heuristics for power-aware scheduling algorithms. This algorithm is used for scheduling jobs with established duties onto the computational cloud. A power-aware scheduling scheme is mentioned that reduces electricity consumption with the aid of altering the status of the computing device to hibernate or offline. The selection is a difficult challenge as each and every answer has its personal set of pros and cons. The implementation with minimal value has the advantage of the lowest electricity consumption; however the response time of the jobs is high. On the other hand, the minimal response heuristics preserve the response time to the lowest with greatest power. One can diagram heuristics that can calculate the trade-offs between the two goal features and assist in choosing an intermediate answer that eliminates each extreme. The fundamental disadvantage of this approach is that it cannot function in an heterogeneous cloud environment. Nikolaos D. Doulamis et al. [13] have proposed a new algorithm for honest scheduling, and it is in contrast with the different scheduling schemes such as the earliest deadline first (EDF) and the first come first served (FCFS) schemes. This algorithm makes use of a max-min truthful sharing method for offering verified access to users. When there is no shortage of resources, this algorithm assigns sufficient computational electricity to every project to end inside its deadline. When there is congestion, the essential notion is to decrease the CPU cores assigned to the duties so that the share of resources that every person receives is proportional to the user's weight. The weight can also be described as the user's contribution to the infrastructure or the fee he is willing to pay for offerings or any other socioeconomic consideration.

10.4 PROBLEM IDENTIFICATION AND PROPOSED SOLUTIONS

Arjun Singh and P. Chakrabarti [14] have proposed an ant-based totally based on discovery and mobility conscious have confidence management for cellular cloud systems. Initially the super-cloud nodes are chosen in the community; the use of ant colony optimization is primarily based on the parameters such as distance, CPU speed, on-hand bandwidth and residual battery power. These chosen nodes are utilized in the useful resource discovery mechanism. In order to strengthen security with the mobility administration system, a knowledge base have popularity collection approach has been adopted [15]. By the simulation results, the creator suggests that the proposed method is environmentally friendly and provides greater security. One necessary difficulty is scheduling the computation duties and the conversation transactions onto the goal architecture when the cellular cloud surroundings and a pre-selected structure are given. This includes:

- Assigning the distribution of duties and conversation transactions onto the specific computation and communication resources, respectively.

- Fixing the order of their execution on these shared resources which is referred to as the scheduling problem. The answer to the scheduling problem has a massive impact on the whole machine strength consumption. Due to the heterogeneity of the architecture, assigning the same challenge to different processing factors leads to very unique computation electricity consumption.

- For special assignments, the inter-task conversation quantity and the routing direction can fluctuate significantly which leads to very exclusive values for the conversation electricity consumption [17–19].

Although the scheduling hassle is a traditional subject matter for research, nearly all current work focuses on maximizing the overall performance via the scheduling process. The algorithms developed are now not appropriate for real-time embedded applications, in which a frequent goal is to limit the power consumption of the device under tight overall performance constraints.

Moreover, most of the present work neglects the inter-processor communication factors at some stage in the scheduling process, or assumes a constant proportional to the communication volume, except thinking about the refined results like the conversation congestion which might also change dynamically for the duration of duty execution. Figure 10.1 suggests the structure of a cellular cloud network.

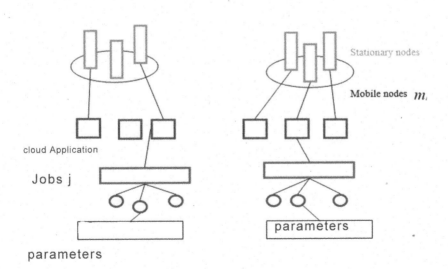

FIGURE 10.1   Architecture of mobile cloud in network.

10.4.1 Estimation of Residual Battery Power

After time t, the power consumed by the node ($P_c(t)$) is computed as follows:

$$P_c(t) = DP_{tx} * a1 + DP_{rx} * a2 \qquad (10.1)$$

Where DP_{tx} = number of data packets transmitted by the node after time t.
DP_{rx} = number of data packets received by the node after time t.

10.4.2 Estimation of Residual Battery Power

After time $t1$, the power used by the device ($P_a(t1)$) is computed as follows:

$$P_a(t1) = D_{ax} * a1 + DP_{rx} * a2 \qquad (10.2)$$

Where DP_{qx} = number of data packets transmitted by the node after time $t1$.
DP_{rx} = number of data packets received by the node after time $t1$.

10.5 HIERARCHICAL TASK SCHEDULING

The profile of nodes contains the following fields:

- Mnid1 (cloud clous node ID).
- Imgsid1 (I-MGS ID).
- Speed1 (device speed).
- no_tasks1 (currently executing tasks).
- wload1 (workload of device).
- power1 (power level of the node).
- ntasks1 (details of current tasks).
- status1 (status of the node).

For each task, the following details are stored:

- Tid1 (task ID).
- Tsize1 (memory size required).
- Exectime1 (execution time).

10.5.1 Algorithm

- Whenever an MN wants to execute a set of tasks $\{Tj, j = 1,2,\ldots,k\}$, it submits the task details to its SGN.

- The SGN estimates the workload of its MNs $\{MNi, i = 1,2,\ldots,n\}$ using the following formula:

- If Pa_i is the opening battery power of a device, the remaining battery power [9] of a device at time ta can be calculated as:

$$Pa_{res} = Pa_i - Pa_c(t1c)$$

$$Wload_{ia} = CWload_{ia} + \left(\sum_{j=1}^{k} tsize_{ja} / power_{ia} \right)$$

- Where $CWload_{ia}$ is the workload of the device.

$$Wload_i a = CWload_{ia} + \left(\sum_{j=1}^{k} tsize_{ja} / power_{ia} \right)$$

- Where $CWload_{ia}$ is the present workload of the device.

- $power_{ia}$ is the power of the device and $tsize_{ja}$ is the size of the task ja.

    So total workload is:

$$TaWload = \sum_{i=1}^{n} Waload_i$$

- Let avg_A is the average workload of the cloud and T is the tolerable limit of the workload.

- If $Wload_{ia} >$ avg + T, then the status of MN_i is observed as OVERLOADED.

- If $Wload_{ia} <$ avg_A, then the status of MN_i is observed as UNDERLOADED.

- If $Wload_{ia} \geq$ avg_A and $Wload_{ia} \leq$ avg_A + T, then the device is labeled as BALANCED.

- Let n_ul, n_ol and n_bl denote the number of underloaded MNs, number of overloaded MNs and number of balanced MNs, respectively.

- Then SGN check the following condition:

  If $ntasks > (n\_ul + n\_bl)$, then split the tasks into subtasks as

$$stask\_A = ntasks/n\_ul + n\_bl$$

Otherwise, don't split the task.

- The SGN assigns the subtasks to the underloaded and balanced MNs only.

- If there are no underloaded and overloaded MNs, the SGN sends a request to another SGN with the details of the remaining tasks to be executed.

- The SGN then forwards this request to another SGN.

- The same process is repeated until all the subtasks are successfully assigned.

- Once the execution of the subtasks is over, the corresponding MNs return the completed task to the requested MN.

- If any one of the assigned MN moves out of the range, then its task is again rescheduled to another MN, in the same way described above.

10.5.2 Algorithm Description

Whenever a MN wishes to execute a set of tasks, it submits the undertaking details to its SGN. The SGN estimates the workload of its MNs with the use of the following formula:

$$Wload_i + \left(\sum_{j=1}^{k} tsize_j/power_i \right)$$

Here workload is represented in terms of the undertaking measurement and battery energy of the cellular node. So the cell node with the least workload and extra battery energy can be chosen to execute the tasks. The status of a cellular node is marked as balanced, overloaded or underloaded depending on the common workload. The status of a cell node is marked as overloaded if the workload is higher than the sum of the common workload and the tolerable restriction of the workload. On the other hand, if the workload is between the common workload and the sum of average workload and the tolerable limit, then the cell node is viewed as balanced. After marking the status of the cellular nodes, the SGN tests whether or not the range of duties is larger than the sum of the variety of underloaded and the range of balanced cell nodes and splits the duties into subtasks. Otherwise, the duties are now not broken up into subtasks. A node is marked as underloaded, if the workload is less than the common workload. The SGN assigns the subtasks to the underloaded and balanced MNs only. If there are no underloaded and overloaded MNs, the SGN sends a request to its I-MGS with the details of the final duties to be executed.

10.6 ADVANTAGES OF THE PROPOSED APPROACH

i. It minimizes the electricity consumption of the cell nodes.

ii. Since it is hierarchical, work can be redistributed or rescheduled.

iii. Since the duties are broken up into subtasks and accomplished in parallel, it reduces the execution time and memory size.

iv. If a cellular node strikes out of range, its assignment can be rescheduled. Here workload is represented.

10.7 SIMULATION

NS2 [20] is used to simulate the proposed algorithm. Figure 10.2 offers the pattern community topology used in the simulation. In this simulation, 30 grid nodes are deployed in a 1,000 meter × 1,000 meter vicinity for 50 seconds' simulation time. Among all of the 30 grid nodes, 20 nodes act as cellular grid nodes (indicated as 'G' in discern 4) and 10 nodes act as extremely good grid nodes (indicated as 'SG' in parent 4). It is assumed that every cell grid node strikes independently with the same common speed. The velocity of the cellular grid node is 2 m/s. All nodes have an equal transmission distance of 250 meters. For service discovery, service-level protocol (SLP) is used. An SLP provider agent is connected to the nodes for imparting the offerings and the SLP agent is connected to the customers asking for the service. In this simulation, consumers send provider requests to the relevant grid nodes. The wonderful grid nodes choose the grid nodes matching the carrier request and assign the duties as per our algorithm.

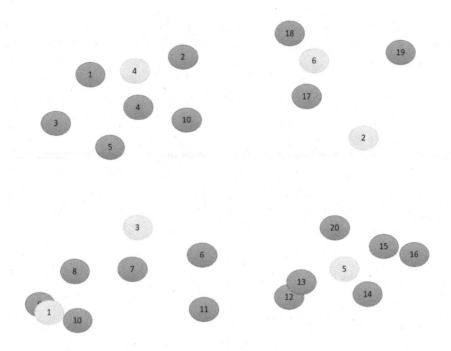

FIGURE 10.2   Simulation topology.

The simulation settings and parameters are summarized in Table 10.1.

A study is shown in terms of the task size and battery power of the cloud node in Table 10.1. So the cloud node with the least workload and more battery power can be selected to execute the tasks. The status of a cloud node is marked as balanced, overloaded or underloaded depending on the average workload. The status of a cloud node is marked as overloaded if the workload is greater than the sum of the average workload and the tolerable limit of the workload. On the other hand, if the workload is between the average workload and the sum of average workload and the tolerable limit, then the cloud node is considered as balanced. After marking the status of the cloud nodes, the SGN checks whether the number of tasks is greater than the sum of the number of underloaded and the number of balanced cloud nodes and splits the tasks into subtasks. Otherwise, the tasks are not split into subtasks. The node is marked as underloaded if the workload is less than the average workload. The SGN assigns the subtasks to the underloaded and balanced MNs only. If there are no underloaded and overloaded MNs, the SGN sends a request to its I-MGS with the details of the remaining tasks to be executed. The energy-constrained hierarchical task scheduling (ECHTS) algorithm is compared with the

TABLE 10.1   Simulation Parameters

Number of grid nodes	20
Number of super grid nodes	10
Area size	1000×1000
Mac	802.11
Radio range	250 m
Simulation time	50 sec
Service discovery protocol	SLP
Server application	SLPsa
Client application	SLPua
Speed	10 m/s
Clients	4
Requested load	10 to 50 kb
Number of requests	1,2,3,4 and 5

EDF technique [13]. According to the following matrices the performance of the algorithm is evaluated:

Average delay: This is measured as the average delay occurring for each client while getting the requested service.

Packet delivery ratio: This is the ratio of the number of nodes for successful data transmission.

Energy consumption: This is the average energy consumed by all the cloud grid nodes.

Throughput: This is the average throughput obtained at the receiver.

10.7.1 Based on the Number of Requests

The number of requests varies from one to five with load 10 kb.

Vary the load of the request from 10 to 50 kb for two requests.

Figure 10.6 shows the delay of ECHTS and EDF techniques for different rate scenarios. We can conclude that the delay of our proposed ECHTS approach is 45% less than the EDF approach.

Figure 10.7 shows the delivery ratio of ECHTS and EDF techniques for different rate scenarios. We can conclude that the delivery ratio of our proposed ECHTS approach is 19% higher than the EDF approach.

Figure 10.8 shows the throughput of ECHTS and EDF techniques for different rate scenarios. We can conclude that the throughput of our proposed ECHTS approach is 18% higher than the EDF approach.

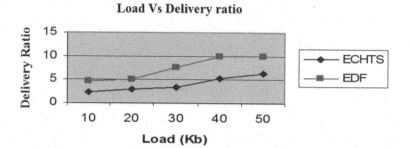

FIGURE 10.3   Request vs delay.

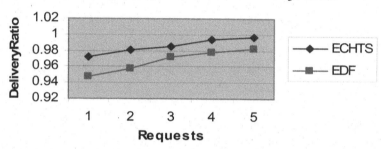

FIGURE 10.4   Request vs delivery ratio.

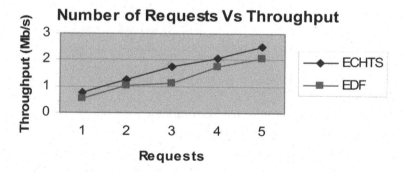

FIGURE 10.5   Request vs throughput.

10.8 CONCLUSION

In this chapter, a strength-limited hierarchical mission scheduling algo-rithm for cloud grids is proposed to decrease the electricity consumption of the cell nodes. The venture is rescheduled when the cell node strikes past the transmission range. Scheduling is essential due to the need to tackle the closing date constraints and device heterogeneity. The overall

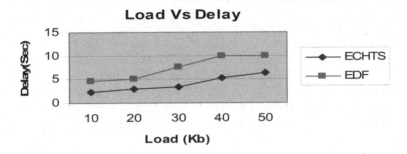

FIGURE 10.6   Load vs delay.

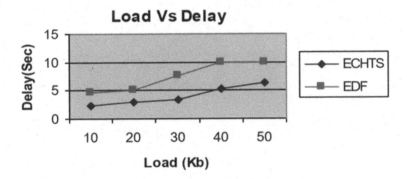

FIGURE 10.7   Load vs delivery ratio.

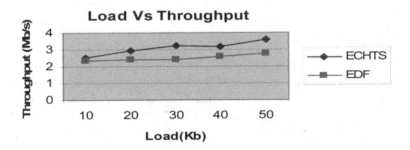

FIGURE 10.8   Load vs throughput.

performance is estimated based totally on the common delay, which is reduced; packet shipping ratio, which is increased; equity and bandwidth, which are barely increased; and power consumption which is lowered primarily based on nodes and flows. By simulation, the overall performance metrics are analyzed with the use of NS-2 simulator.

REFERENCES

1. Rodriguez Juan Manuel, Alejandro Zunino, and Marcelo Campo "Cloud grid seas: simple energy-aware scheduler," in Proceedings of the 3rd High-Performance Computing Symposium-39th JAIIO, 2010.
2. Ghosh, Preetam, Nirmalya Roy, Sajal K. Das, and Kalyan Basu "A game theory based pricing strategy for job allocation in cloud grids," in Proceedings of the 18th International Parallel and Distributed Processing Symposium, p. 82. IEEE, 2004.
3. Li, Chunlin, and Layuan Li "Simultaneous optimization of application utility and consumed energy in cloud grid," *Computing and Informatics*, 29.6 (2012): 1117–1140.
4. Ghosh, Preetam, et al. "A pricing strategy for job allocation in cloud grids using a non-cooperative bargaining theory framework," *Journal of Parallel and Distributed Computing*, 65.11 (2005): 1366–1383.
5. Sim, Kwang Mong "A survey of bargaining models for grid resource allocation," *ACM SIGecom Exchanges*, 5.5 (2006): 22–32.
6. Khan, Samee Ullah, and Cemal Ardil "Energy efficient resource allocation in distributed computing systems," in International Conference on Distributed, High-Performance and Grid Computing, 2009.
7. Prosperi, Francesco, Mario Bambagini, Giorgio Buttazzo, Mauro Marinoni, and Gianluca Franchino. "Energy-aware algorithms for tasks and bandwidth co-allocation under real-time and redundancy constraints." In Proceedings of 2012 IEEE 17th International Conference on Emerging Technologies & Factory Automation (ETFA 2012), pp. 1–8. IEEE, 2012.
8. Kim, Jong-Kook, Howard Jay Siegel, Anthony A. Maciejewski, and Rudolf Eigenmann. "Dynamic resource management in energy constrained heterogeneous computing systems using voltage scaling," *IEEE Transactions on Parallel and Distributed Systems*, 19.11 (2008): 1445–1457.
9. Tekbiyik, Neyre, Tolga Girici, Elif Uysal-Biyikoglu, and Kemal Leblebicioglu. "Proportional fair resource allocation on an energy harvesting downlink-part II: algorithms," arXiv preprint arXiv:1205.5153 (2012).
10. Malla, Samip, Birendra Ghimire, Mark C. Reed, and Harald Haas. "Energy efficient resource allocation in OFDMA networks using ant-colony optimization," in International Symposium on Communications and Information Technologies (ISCIT), 2012, pp. 889–894, IEEE, 2012.
11. Li, Chunlin, and Layuan Li. "Energy constrained resource allocation optimization for cloud grids," Elsevier, 2009.
12. Aziz, Abdul, and Hesham El-Rewini, *Power Efficient Scheduling Heuristics for Energy Conservation in Computational Grids*, Springer, 2011.
13. Doulamis, Nikolaos D., Anastasios D. Doulamis, Emmanouel A. Varvarigos, and Theodora A. Varvarigou. "Fair scheduling algorithms in grids," *IEEE Transactions on Parallel and Distributed Systems*, 18.11 (2007): 1630–1648.
14. Singh Arjun, and Chakrabarti P. "Ant based resource discovery and mobility aware trust management for cloud grid systems," in IACC IEEE 3rd International Conference, pp. 637–644, Feb 2013.

15. Preetam Ghosh, and Sajal K. Das. "Mobility-aware cost-efficient job scheduling for single class grid jobs in a generic cloud grid architecture," *Future Generation Computer Systems*, In Press, Corrected Proof, 2009.

16. Chunlin Li, and Layuan Li. "Energy constrained resource allocation optimization for cloud grids," *Journal of Parallel and Distributed Computing* 70.3 (2010): 245–258.

17. W. X. Shen, C. C. Chan, E.W. C. Lo, and K. T. Chau. "Estimation of battery available capacity under variable discharge currents," *Journal of Power Sources* 103.2 (2002): 180–187.

18. Ming-Chiao Chen, Jiann-Liang Chen, and Teng-Wen Chang. "Android/osgi-based vehicular network management system," *Computer Communications*, In Press, Corrected Proof, 2010.

19. Ashish Agarwal, Douglas O. Norman, and Amar Gupta "Wireless grids: Approaches, architectures, and technical challenges," *Working Chapters 4459–04*, Massachusetts Institute of Technology (MIT), Sloan School of Management, 2004.

20. Network Simulator: http:///www.isi.edu/nsnam/ns

Index